TRIBAL LAWS,
TREATIES, AND
GOVERNMENT

A LAKOTA PERSPECTIVE

TRIBAL LAWS, **TREATIES,** AND GOVERNMENT

A LAKOTA PERSPECTIVE

PATRICK A. LEE
EDITED BY CHRISTOPHER K. BAKER

iUniverse, Inc.
Bloomington

Tribal Laws, Treaties, and Government
A Lakota Perspective

iUniverse books may be ordered through booksellers or by contacting:

iUniverse
1663 Liberty Drive
Bloomington, IN 47403
www.iuniverse.com
1-800-Authors (1-800-288-4677)

ISBN: 978-1-4759-8686-0 (sc)
ISBN: 978-1-4759-8687-7 (ebk)

Printed in the United States of America

iUniverse rev. date: 06/11/2013

TABLE OF CONTENTS

INTRODUCTION

Tribal Laws. Treaties and Government is a very popular undergraduate course offered at Oglala Lakota College and other tribal colleges. The topic is much more than an academic subject because it addresses current as well as past issues resulting from the history of tribal and U.S. relations that evolved over the years. Its popularity is based on student and community interest in treaties and treaty law. The traditional Lakota Treaty Council exists along with the Oglala Sioux Tribal Council. These organizations trace their respective powers back to the times leading up to the Fort Laramie Treaty of 1851 followed by the Fort Laramie Treaty of 1868. The fundamental treaty and national rights of sovereignty are embedded in the treaties made with the United States by the Lakota and other Indian nations.

This course has been offered for many years without a specific textbook. The material contained in this textbook replaces the collection of compiled materials that has been in use by OLC. This textbook contains the substance of the lectures and discussions that developed over the past thirty years of teaching the Lakota perspective of treaties, treaty case law, tribal law, federal Indian laws, Supreme Court cases impacting Indian tribes and the federal Indian policy underlying a given law or court decision. The complexities of the issues and the legal analyses required for understanding the issues creates a need for a simplified, detailed, but comprehensive textbook for instruction in the areas of treaties, treaty law, federal law about Indian and tribal law.

Relations between the Lakota and the United States have caused much resentment among the Lakota and other Indian nations against the United States. The formation of the American Indian Movement (AIM), the 1969 "Indians of All Tribes" occupation of Alcatraz, the 1972 "Trail of Broken Treaties" leading to the occupation of the BIA building in Washington D.C. and the 1973 Wounded Knee Occupation on the Pine Ridge Indian Reservation are all connected to the failure of the United States to honor its treaties with Indian nations and subsequent atrocities committed against Indians. Especially disconcerting to the Lakota nations is the confiscation of the Black Hills in South Dakota by the United States from the treaty tribes in violation of its solemn treaty commitments. The fact that Shannon County, on the Pine Ridge Indian Reservation is the poorest county in the nation is alarming when one considers the value of the Black Hills that the Lakota reserved in the 1868 Fort Laramie Treaty. The Black Hills is the most valuable land area in the United States in terms of mineral, timber, and natural resources. This book is based on the Lakota perspective and there has been no attempt to sugarcoat the atrocities that occurred as a result of treaty violations by the United States.

CHAPTER ONE

TREATY-MAKING

Webster's Dictionary defines a treaty as a formal agreement between two or more nations, relating to peace, alliance, and a document embodying such an agreement.

Treaties are agreements between sovereign nations. Each party to a treaty recognizes and acknowledges the other as a sovereign nation. A treaty is internationally-based, and is grounded on trust and a solemn belief that each party will uphold the promises and commitments made to one another. Sovereign nations are those communities that possess all or most of the attributes of sovereignty, including its territory, citizens, government, laws or customs, its distinct culture and its right to manage its own affairs.

When the British and Europeans settled on the east coast of North America, Great Britain began dealing with Indians by making treaties with them. The original English colonies were feeble settlements, and the natives in that area helped the colonists by teaching them to survive in the natural world by teaching them the indigenous arts of hunting, gathering, and planting. The Indians of the east coast were integral in the colonists' ability to sustain themselves.

The colonies eventually revolted against Great Britain and became the United States of America. The colonies were converted to states within the new nation. As the colonial populations flourished and grew in numbers they demanded more and more land. The United States adopted the policy of Great Britain and began making treaties with the Indian nations. The first U.S. Indian treaty was made in 1778 with the Delaware Nation.

The first U.S.—Indian treaties were made for the purpose of acquiring land, and for validating land acquisitions. Other European nations would recognize treaties made by the United States and Indian nations, would acknowledge them, and would not likely interfere with the United States' interest in lands it acquired from Indian nations.[1] The treaties that followed were all acquired for virtually the same purposes—land for roads, stage stations, railroads, towns, settlers, etc. Anthropologist Raymond DeMallie has found other motives of the United States in making treaties with Indian nations. In addition to validating land claims of the United States against European powers, the United States wished to establish trade with Indian nations that would protect the interests of U.S. merchants and manufacturers. As the United States acquired land from the Indian nations, a portion of the Indian land would be set aside for the Indians to occupy. This land was left in reserve for the use and occupation of the Indians; hence, the term "Indian Reservation" meant that Indians would continue to occupy land set aside or reserved for their use. The United States also was motivated to keep Indians on Indian reservations and to resolve the so-called "Indian problem". History shows that once the treaties were signed, the so-called "Indian problem" was not resolved for the whites, because the Indians continued to occupy the land reserved for them. What turned out to be a problem was that the whites were not satisfied with the Indians' continued occupancy of their land, but wanted more of the land than had been agreed to in the treaty. Hence the real problem turned out to be a "white problem" for the Indians.

In 1830 the Cherokee Nation filed a lawsuit against the State of Georgia for enforcing its laws on the Cherokee Indian Reservation. The Cherokees argued that because each Cherokee Indian was not a U.S. citizen, it qualified as a foreign nation and was allowed to file the original complaint in the Supreme Court of the United States. The Supreme Court disagreed that the Cherokees constituted a "foreign" nation, but concluded that an Indian nation is a domestic dependent nation. Chief Justice John Marshall reasoned that the relationship between Indian nations and the United States was unique in that it resembled that of a ward to his guardian. While the Cherokee nation was comprised of all the elements of a nation, the Court held that a domestic dependent nation is not a foreign nation within the meaning of the constitution and that the Supreme Court did not have original jurisdiction to hear the case. It would have to be refiled in a lower court and brought to the Supreme Court on appeal. The case was resolved two years later, however, when Samuel Worcester, a missionary from Vermont appealed his conviction by a Georgia court for residing on the Cherokee reservation without a license from the State of Georgia. Worcester was sentenced to serve four years in the state penitentiary. On appeal, the U.S. Supreme Court reversed the Georgia court and ruled that state law does not apply on Indian land. President Andrew Jackson is credited with remarking that: "John Marshall made his decision, now let him enforce it." The Governor of Georgia pardoned Samuel Worcester and he was released from the state prison. The case stands for the rule of law

---

[1] American Indian Treaty Making: Motives and Meanings. Raymond DeMallie, Institute for the Development of Indian Law, Inc. Lawton, Oklahoma

that state law has no force or effect on Indian reservations. This precedent applied to all other Indian reservations throughout the United States.

Discovery of gold in the west proved to be problematic, if not catastrophic, for Native Americans. The California Gold Rush of 1849 created a need for the United States to establish safe passage for its citizens to travel westward, through Indian country to northern California and southern Oregon. The presence of miners, trappers, hunters, and fur traders in the Fort Laramie area raised the concerns of Indian Agent Thomas Fitzpatrick, who recommended to his Superintendent, D. D. Mitchell, that the United States meet with the Plains Indians to discuss the proposed right-of-way through their country. Congress responded in February 1851 by allocating $100,000 for treaty negotiations with the Plains Indians. The primary motive of the United States in making the Fort Laramie Treaty of 1851 was to secure safe passage for U.S. citizens to travel through central North America by way of the Oregon Trail, which wound its way through the plains, hills, and mountains with its final destination being the gold fields of northern California. By making the treaty with the plains Indians in 1851, the United States formally recognized that the various Indian nations in the area held a valid aboriginal title to the land they owned and occupied. The fact that the United States had "purchased" the area in 1803 from France did nothing to diminish the legality of the aboriginal title held by the various Indian nations occupying the land.

The Fort Laramie Treaty of 1851 included virtually all of the mid-western Native Nations.

CHAPTER TWO

"TREATY OF FORT LARAMIE WITH SIOUX, ETC" (1851)

"Articles of a treaty made and concluded at Fort Laramie, in the Indian Territory, between D. D. Mitchell, superintendent of Indian affairs, and Thomas Fitzpatrick, Indian agent commissioners specially appointed and authorized by the President of the United States, of the first part, and the chiefs, headmen, and braves of the following Indian nations, residing south of the Missouri River, east of the Rocky Mountains, and north of the lines of Texas and New Mexico, viz, the Sioux or Dacotahs, Cheyennes, Arrapahoes, Crows, Assinaboines, Gros-Ventre, Mandans, and Arrickaras, parties of the second part on the seventeenth day of September A.D. one thousand eight hundred and fifty-one.

"Article 1. The aforesaid nations, parties to this treaty having assembled for the purpose of establishing and confirming peaceful relations amongst themselves, do hereby covenant and agree to abstain in the future from all hostilities whatever against each other, to maintain good faith and friendship in all their mutual intercourse, and to make an effective and lasting peace.

"Article 2. The aforesaid nations do hereby recognize the right of the United State Government to establish roads, military and other posts, within their respective territories.

"Article 3. In consideration of the rights and privileges acknowledged in the preceding article, the United States bind themselves to protect the aforesaid Indian nations against the commission of all depredations by the people of the said United States after ratification of this treaty.

"Article 4. The aforesaid Indian nations do hereby agree to bind themselves to make restitution or satisfaction for any wrongs committed, after the ratification of this treaty, by any band or individual of their people, on the people of the United States, while lawfully residing in or passing through their respective territories.

"Article 5. The aforesaid Indian nations do hereby recognize and acknowledge the following tracts of country included within the metes and boundaries hereinafter designated, as their respective territories, viz: "The territory of the Sioux or Dacotah Nation, commencing at the mouth of the White Earth River, on the Missouri River; thence in a southwesterly direction to the forks of the Platte River to a point known as the Red Butte, or where the road leaves the river; thence along the range of mountains known as the Black Hills, to the headwaters of the Heart River; thence down Heart River to its mouth; and thence down the Missouri River to the place of the beginning."

"The territory of the Gros Ventre, Mandan, and Arrickara Nations, commencing at the mouth of the Heart River; thence up the Missouri River to the mouth of the Yellowstone River; thence up the Yellowstone River to the mouth of the Powder River in a southeasterly direction, to the head-waters of the Little Missouri River; thence along the Black Hills to the head of the Heart River, and thence down Heart River to the place of the beginning."

"The territory of the Assiniboine Nation, commencing at the mouth of the Yellowstone River; thence up the Missouri River to the mouth of the Muscle-shell River; thence from the mouth of the Muscle-shell River in a southeasterly direction until it strikes the head-waters of the Big Dry Creek; thence down that creek to where it empties into the Yellowstone River; nearly opposite the mouth of Powder River, and thence down the Yellowstone River to the place of the beginning."

"The territory of the Blackfoot Nation, commencing at the mouth of Muscle-shell River; thence up the Missouri River to its source; thence along the main range of the Rocky Mountains, in a southerly direction, to the head-waters of the northern source of the Yellowstone River; thence down the Yellowstone River to the mouth of Twenty-five Yard Creek; thence across to the head-waters of the Muscle-shell River, and thence down the Muscle-shell River to the place of beginning."

"The territory of the Crow Nation, commencing at the mouth of Powder River on the Yellowstone; thence up Powder River to its source; thence along the main range of the Black Hills and Wind River Mountains to the head-waters of the Yellowstone River; thence down the Yellowstone River to the mouth of Twenty-five Yard Creek; thence to the head waters of the Muscle-shell River; thence down the

Muscle-shell River to its mouth; thence to the head-waters of Big Cry Creek, and thence to its mouth."

"The territory of the Cheyennes and Arapahos. Commencing at the Red Butte, or the place where the road leaves the north fork of the Platte River; thence up the north fork of the Platte River to its source; thence along the main range of the Rocky Mountains to the head-waters of the Arkansas River; thence down the Arkansas River to the crossing of the Santa Fe' road; thence in a northwesterly direction to the forks of the Platte River, and thence up the Platte River to the place of beginning."

"It is however, understood that, in making this recognition and acknowledgment, the aforesaid Indian nations do not hereby abandon or prejudice any rights or claims they may have to other lands; and further, that they do not surrender the privilege of hunting, fishing or passing over any of the tracts of country heretofore described.

"Article 6. The parties to the second part of this treaty having selected principals or head chiefs for their respective nations, through whom all national business will hereafter be conducted, do hereby bind themselves to sustain said chiefs and their successors during good behavior.

"Article 7. In consideration of the treaty stipulations and for the damages which have or may occur by reason hereof to the Indian nations, parties hereto, and for their maintenance and the improvement of their moral and social customs, the Unites States bind themselves to deliver to the said Indian nations the sum of fifty thousand dollars per annum for the term of ten years, with the right to continue the same at the discretion of the President of the United States for a period not exceeding five years thereafter, in provisions, merchandise, domestic animals, and agricultural implements, in such proportions as may be deemed best adapted to their condition by the President of the United states, to be distributed in proportion to the population of the aforesaid Indian nations.

"Article 8. It is understood and agreed that should any of the Indian nations, parties to this treaty, violate any of the provisions thereof, the United States may withhold the whole or a portion of the annuities mentioned in the preceding article from the nation so offending, until in the opinion of the President of the United States, proper satisfaction shall have been made.

"In testimony whereof the said D. D. Mitchell and Thomas Fitzpatrick, commissioners as aforesaid, and the chiefs, headmen, and braves, parties hereto,

have set their hands and affixed their marks, on the day and at the place first written."

D. D. Mitchell

Thomas Fitzpatrick,

Commissioners.

Sioux:

Mah-toe-wha-you-whey, his x mark,

Mah-kah-toe-zah-zah, his x mark

Belon-o-ton-kah-tan-go, his x mark

Nah-kapah-gi-gi, his x mark

Mak-toe-sah-bi-chis, his x mark

Meh-wha-tah-ni-hans-kah, his x mark

Cheyennes:

Wah-ha-nis-satta, his x mark,

Voist-ti-toe-vetz, his x mark

Nahk-ko-me-ien, his x mark

Koh-kah-y-wh-cum-est, his x mark

Crows:

Arra-tu-ri-sah, his x mark,

Doh-chepit-she, che-es, his mark

Assinaboines:

Mah-to-wit-ko, his x mark

Toe-tah-ki=eh-nan- his x mark

Mandans and Gros Ventres:

Nochk-pit-shi-toe-pish, his x mark

She-oh-mant-ho, his mark

Arickarees:

Koun-hei-ti-shan, his x mark

Bi-atch-tah-wetch, his x mark

In the presence of ---

A,B. Chambers, secretary

S. Cooper, colonel, U.S. Army

R.H. Chilton, captain First Drags

Thomas Duncan, captain, Mounted Riflemen

Thos. G. Rhett, brevet captain R. M. R.

W. L. Elliott, first lieutenant R. M. R.

C. Campbell, interpreter for Sioux

John S. Smith, interpreter for Cheyenne

Robert Meldrum interpreter for Crows

H. Culbertson interpreter for Assiniboine

and Gros Ventres.

Francois L'Estalie, interpreter for Arickarees

John Pizelle, interpreter for Arapahoe

B. Gratz Brown.

Robert Campbell.

Edward F. Chouteau.

The Fort Laramie Treaty of 1851 recognized and acknowledged the fact that the Lakota Sioux owned and occupied all of western South Dakota and large portions of Nebraska, Wyoming and Montana. In exchange for permission for travelers on the Oregon Trail to safely pass through this area, the United States made the aforementioned promises and concessions.

The Fort Laramie Treaty of 1851 afforded the Plains Indians with access to traders and to collect rations from the United States principally at Fort Laramie. This enabled the Indians to acquire manufactured goods and to continue trade for the purpose of acquiring metal tools, weapons, guns and ammunition. DeMallie also points out some common misunderstandings among the Indians and the whites. The whites immediately assumed that a "chief" was empowered to sign a treaty on behalf of an Indian nation and that the treaty would automatically be binding on the entire Indian nation. The whites considered the chief to be the equivalent of the President, or Chief Executive of the United States. To the Indians, the signing of a treaty by a chief simply meant that one person agreed to a treaty and that the treaty was not binding on the entire Indian nation. No one chief had the power to sign a treaty on behalf of the entire Indian nation. There were many chiefs, each with a role that was unique to that chief. A war chief had certain duties aside from political activities. A medicine man was considered a chief for the purpose of performing spiritual healing practices. Each band of the Lakota had certain chiefs that had no power or authority over other Lakota bands. One band would not recognize and accept the signing of a treaty by a chief of another band. A good example of this social structure occurred when a group of Mormons was passing by Fort Laramie in the year, 1854. A lame cow belonging to the Mormon group straggled into Chief Conquering Bear's Sicangu—Brule' camp, which was situated just outside of Fort Laramie. A visiting warrior from the Minniconjou band by the name of Straight Foretop killed and butchered the lame cow. The Mormon complained to the military at Fort Laramie that someone in Conquering Bear's camp stole the Mormon's cow. The officer in charge, Lieutenant Grattan took thirty soldiers and two canons to Conquering Bear's village and demanded that the warrior be turned over to the military. Conquering Bear explained to Lt. Grattan that Straight Foretop was a Minniconjou Lakota and that he, a Sicangu chief, had no authority to give orders to Straight Foretop. Lt. Grattan refused to listen. He issued an ultimatum, which was not met. He then ordered his men to fire their canons on Conquering Bear's camp, which they did. Many in Conquering Bear's camp were killed and Conquering Bear was mortally wounded. A larger group of Lakota warriors were watching from the hillsides and immediately charged Lt. Grattan's troops and killed Lt. Grattan and all thirty of his soldiers. Conquering Bear died a few days later from his wounds.

An investigation of the incident later disclosed that Lt. Grattan had acted improperly. The earlier Fort Laramie Treaty of 1851 did not authorize the military to arrest any Indian who committed depredations against the whites, but provided instead that restitution should be made. Chief Conquering Bear had offered to pay ten dollars or one of his prize ponies to replace the lame cow. Lt. Grattan refused the offer even though the cow belonged to the Mormons. Despite the fact that Lt. Grattan instigated the confrontation and was in violation of the treaty, the United States used the battle as a pretext for additional military actions against the Lakota on Lakota land.

The Grattan treaty violation occurred only three years after the signing of the Fort Laramie Treaty of 1851. One year after the death of Conquering Bear, General William S. Harney led a troop of 1200 men to Fort Laramie seeking revenge for the Grattan battle. He met with Chief Little Thunder who was meeting at Ash Hollow, which was a few miles east of Fort Laramie, with family groups of Oglala and Brule encampments. The Indians were present at Fort Laramie for the purpose of trading. Lakota families of men, women and children were present. While Little Thunder and Harney were meeting, Harney's men opened fire on the villages and killed over eighty people, many of them women and children of the Oglala and Brule bands. Another seventy women with children were captured and taken to Fort Laramie. Brule Chief Spotted Tail agreed to surrender to the U.S. Army in exchange for the release of the women and children of the two camps. Spotted Tail, along with Long Chin and Red Leaf were taken as hostages to Fort Leavenworth, Kansas. South Dakota historian Will Robinson described the brutality of General Harney by writing, "Though hailed as a great victory and an additional plume in Harney's crest of fame, the battle of Ash Hollow was a shameful affair, unworthy of American arms and a disgrace to the officer who planned and executed it. The Indians were trapped and knew it and would have surrendered at discretion had an opportunity been afforded them. That opportunity was not given, and the massacre which ensued was as needless and as barbarous as any which the Dakotas have at any time visited upon the white people."[22]

While the President of the United States has the constitutional authority to sign a treaty, and the Senate's role is to ratify a treaty signed by the President, there is no such formality among the Lakota. The whites simply refused to recognize the social structure of the Lakota and expected the Lakota to follow the political protocol of the whites. This misunderstanding caused problems that resulted in the loss of more Lakota lives and property.

One special problem cited by DeMallie involves the legal effect of a treaty. To the whites, a treaty once approved has all the requirements of a legally binding document. It is a document that is enforceable by the offended party in a court of law if necessary. To the Indians, the treaty at that time was nothing more than a piece of paper with abstract scratches and markings on it. The whites presented the paper to them, described what it meant, smoked the pipe with them and signed the paper in their presence. In polite consideration the Indians would put their marks on the document as a gesture of friendship and camaraderie. The meeting was amicable; there was good conversation and the exchange of presents. A formal legally enforceable document was not in the minds of the Lakota during the treaty period.

Over the years, it appears that the parties have switched attitudes toward a formally executed treaty. History shows that the Indians have taken the view that these treaties are legally binding documents to be enforced by the offended party in a court of law, if necessary. On the other hand, history shows that it is the whites that now view a treaty simply as a piece of paper with dates and signatures which can be ignored and abrogated at the will of the whites. As to the enforceability of a treaty, the United States recognized the binding effect of a treaty on the Indians who gave up their land, but when it came to the United States upholding its end of the treaty, it was literally just a piece of paper to be ignored. Enforcement of a treaty through court action was a legal impossibility until the twentieth century. In 1903 the Supreme Court held that Congress could abrogate a treaty at will, because it has plenary power to regulate commerce among the Indian tribes. (*Lone Wolf v. Hitchcock*).

A larger problem is the fact that the only courts of law that are available to the Lakota are the U.S. courts. When the government violates a treaty, the Indian nation is expected to seek justice in a government court if the government allows itself to be sued.

---

[2]   Dakota Indian Treaties, From Nomad to Reservation, Don C. Clowser p. 40

The government is protected by "sovereign immunity" and cannot be sued unless that immunity is waived. The government did not allow Indian tribes to pursue legal court action until 1920. There are very few federal treaty cases wherein the Indian tribe has prevailed. There are many injustices handed out by U.S. courts to the detriment of Indian nations who attempt to seek justice against the United States for treaty violations. There are no neutral courts where the Lakota might seek real justice. The *Lone Wolf* case opened the door for more treaty violations, which lasted throughout the 19th century and into the 20th century. In 1920 Congress finally waived its sovereign immunity and allowed the Sioux Nation tribes to file lawsuits in the U.S. Court of Claims over treaty violations. The only remedy allowed, however, is a monetary judgment award. It is still legally impossible to recover Indian land that was stolen as a result of a treaty violation.

CHAPTER THREE

THE BOZEMAN TRAIL

In 1861, a mere ten years after the Fort Laramie Treaty of 1851 proclaimed lands west of the Black Hills to be Sioux Country, gold was discovered in Montana. As gold attracted miners to California, the same yellow mineral proved to be a magnet attracting thousands of miners to Virginia City, Montana. Finding one's way to Montana was no easy task if a prospector wanted to avoid trespassing through Sioux land. For example, one could travel up the Missouri River to Fort Hall, Idaho, and double back to Montana without traveling through Indian country. That route was not acceptable to the likes of John Bozeman, a Mormon explorer, who blazed a trail through the prime Sioux hunting grounds that stretched from the Powder River country west of the Black Hills to the east of the Big Horn Mountains. The road was a blatant violation of the Fort Laramie Treaty. The government had promised in the Fort Laramie Treaty to protect the Indians from depredations. Article 3 of the treaty provides that "In consideration of the rights and privileges acknowledged in the preceding article, the United States bind themselves to protect the aforesaid Indian nations against the commission of all depredations by the people of the United States, after ratification of this treaty." "Depredation" is defined as "the act or an instance of robbing, plundering, or laying waste." (Webster's Dictionary)

Up to this point the treaty had been broken at least three times. Lt. Grattan's 1854 destruction of the Conquering Bear camp followed by Harney's 1855 plundering of the Little Thunder camp were two previous violations of the treaty, and in 1865 Congress passed a Joint Resolution to appropriate money for the construction of two roads from the Platte River to the Montana gold fields.

Thus the government, the army, and the travelers, were all in violation of the treaty and were guilty of committing depredations against the Lakota. Instead of protecting the Sioux against depredations as promised in the treaty, the United States authorized the construction of forts along the Bozeman Trail, which were used by the U.S. Cavalry to protect the settlers who trespassed through Sioux country on their way to the Montana gold fields.

Oglala Chief Red Cloud was the main player in the Powder River battles. Red Cloud's Oglalas were joined by the Brule', Hunkpapa, Minnicojou and other bands of the Teton Sioux. In the 1930's and 40's the Powder River battles provided a historical setting for Hollywood cowboy and Indian movies. A typical scene involves a wagon train traveling across the prairies as a band of warriors approaches from the hillsides. The wagon master would typically yell, "Form a circle!" and the Indians would swoop down on the travelers. The Indians then ride around the circle of wagons until trumpets blare in the distance and a troop of Cavalry would come charging from the hillsides, and the Indians would then retreat. These historical events were used as props for later Hollywood movies that depicted the Indians as "savages" or "hostiles" and the trespassers as victims. Of course there was never a mention that the battles occurred on Indian land and that the wagon trains were trespassing through Indian country.

The United States was embroiled in its civil war during the years 1861-1865. In 1865 Congress approved the Act of March 3, 1865 that authorized the Department of the Interior to establish four new wagon roads through Sioux territory. The most prominent road was that which branched off the Oregon Trail west of Fort Laramie—the Bozeman Trail. This infraction of the treaty was the reason for the battles in Powder River.

On December 21, 1866, Captain Fetterman met his demise at the hands of Chief Man Afraid of his Horses, Chief Red Cloud, and a young War Chief named Crazy Horse. Crazy Horse sent a small group of warriors toward Fetterman who attacked them, thinking he had them outnumbered. A larger group of Oglala, Hunkpapa and Brule' warriors overwhelmed and killed all eighty soldiers and one officer, Captain Fetterman. It was Fetterman who had boasted that with eighty men he could ride through the entire Sioux Nation.

Following the Fetterman battle U, S. Commissioners including General A. Sully, J.B. Sanborn, N.B. Buford, Colonel E. S. Parker and J.F. Kinney and G. P Beauvais submitted several reports, which included the following:

"In the opinion of this office the statement and facts presented in the report of the commissioners referred to, show the origin of the hostilities in the Platte country to have been principally, if not altogether, the opening of a road for travel by emigrants, miners, and others, from Fort Laramie to Montana, through the hunting grounds of the Indians; the march of troops in July 1866, towards that country which was regarded by some of the chiefs as a declaration of war, and the manner in which the treaty at Fort Laramie in 1866, one of its chief objects being to secure that road, was negotiated. Some of the most influential chiefs refused to sign it and in displeasure left the council. The making of the treaty impressed the military and citizens with the belief that the road in question was safe, and parties unprepared to defend themselves sought to pass over it, but were resisted and driven back with the loss of a number of lives and much property. It has been conclusively ascertained that the Indians engaged in the several acts of hostility committed north of the Platte belongs to the Minneconjou, Brule and Oglala bands of the Sioux, northern Arapahos and Cheyenne, aided by young men from other bands whose impelling motive, doubtless was the desire of plunder and of fame as brave warriors . . ."

The Bozeman Trail began at Fort Laramie, and was a shortcut from Fort Laramie through Indian country to the gold fields of Montana. The road itself was in violation of the Fort Laramie Treaty and led to Indian attacks on forts and wagon trains. In 1867 Congress authorized the President of the United States to appoint a commission consisting of three army officers; namely, N.G. Taylor, Commissioner of Indian Affairs of the Senate, S.S Tappan, and John B. Sanborn for the purpose of establishing peace. After the commission was appointed, another Powder River battle broke out. The Wagon Box Fight was a victory for the Cavalry who lost three soldiers. Indian casualties, however, were numerous. By this time the Wells Fargo Company had sent more than one hundred wagon trains of supplies to the Forts on the Bozeman Trail. Three of the wagons were attacked. The Cavalry had recently acquired the new Springfield breechloader, which enabled them to fire many more volleys than the Indians expected.

On August 6, 1867, the commissioners met at St. Louis. The Lakota agreed to meet the commissioners at Fort Laramie. Red Cloud, his Oglala followers and the Brule Sioux left Fort Laramie. Before leaving, Red Cloud met with General Sherman who said, "We have heard your words, and have thought of them all night, and now give you our answers. You tell us that the building of the railroad, up the Smoky Hill and the wagon road by Power River as the principal causes of the present trouble . . . The Power River road was established last year for the purpose of hauling flour, coffee, and sugar to our people who are digging gold in Montana. No white settlements have been made along the road, nor does the travel there disturb the buffalo, nor does it destroy the elk and antelope. The Indians were permitted to hunt them as usual . . . but if on examination at Laramie, we find the Indian right to be good, we will give it up or pay you for it if you keep the peace . . ." Red Cloud sent word that he would meet with the commission the following spring of 1868. (Dakota Indian Treaties, by Don C. Clowser)

The United States desired peace as well as the Lakota. The government had been through the Civil War, which was very costly in terms of lives and resources. The Lakota experienced a huge loss of buffalo due to the migration of travelers, hunters and traders. The fur trade had created a great demand for buffalo hides. The vast majority of the buffalo were killed for their hides and the meat was left to rot. The buffalo had been the source of food, clothing, and shelter for the Lakota, as well as a spiritual and cultural source.

Chief Spotted Tail was willing to make peace with the United States after his incarceration at Leavenworth. While traveling back to Lakota land, he observed the great numbers of whites who had settled the area north of Kansas to the Dakotas. He then surmised that the sheer number of the whites would eventually require a peaceful solution to the white problem.

CHAPTER FOUR

FORT LARAMIE TREATY OF 1868

The commissioners assembled at Fort Laramie beginning in April through November 1868. On April 29, 1868, the Brule band signed the treaty. Included among the Brule who signed in April were Spotted Tail, Iron Shell, Red Leaf, Black Horn, Bad Left Hand and others. On May 25 the treaty was signed by several Oglala including Man Afraid of His Horses, White Hawk, Black Hawk, Black Tiger, Bad Wound, Grass, American Horse, High Wolf and others. Other signers included the Hunkpapa, Blackfeet, Cutheads, Two Kettle, Sans Arc, and the Santee bands. On May 26 the Minneconjou, Yanktonais, and Arapahoe signed the treaty. Red Cloud, Thunder Man, Iron Cane, High Eagle, Man Afraid and Thunder Flying Running signed on November 6, 1868. Red Cloud and his followers refused to sign until he was assured that the Bozeman Trail would be closed off and that the forts along the Bozeman Trail were abandoned.

The Fort Laramie Treaty of 1868 is appended to this publication in its entirety with the names of the United States representatives, the interpreters and the names of those Lakota chiefs and headmen who signed the treaty. The treaty contains 17 articles as follows:

"**Article 1—From this day forward all war between the parties to this agreement shall forever cease. The Government of the United States desires peace, and its honor is hereby pledged to keep it. The Indians desire peace and they now pledge their honor to maintain it.**

If bad men among the whites, or among other people subject to the authority of the United States shall commit any wrong upon the person or property of the Indians, the United States will, upon proof made to the agent and forwarded to the Commissioner of Indian Affairs at Washington city, proceed at once to cause the offender to be arrested and punished according to the laws of the United States, and also reimburse the injured persons for the loss sustained."

"If bad men among the Indians shall commit a wrong or depredation upon the person or property of anyone, white, black, or Indian, subject to the authority of the United States and at peace therewith, the Indians herein named solemnly agree that they will, upon proof made to their agent, and notice by him, deliver up the wrongdoer to the United States, to be tried and punished according to its laws and, in case they willfully refuse to do so, the person injured shall be reimbursed for his loss from the annuities, or other moneys due or to become due to them under this or other treaties made with the United States; and the President, on advising with the Commissioner of Indian Affairs, shall prescribe such rules and regulations for ascertaining damages under the provisions of this article as in his judgment may be proper, but no one sustaining loss while violating the provisions of this treaty, or the laws of the United States, shall be reimbursed therefore."

When Chief Crow Dog killed Chief Spotted Tail in 1883, he had no idea that his case would have an impact on every Indian reservation in the United States. The Government of the United States relied on Article 1, "bad men among the Indians" clause to prosecute Crow Dog in federal court. The General Crimes Act of the United States extended to Indian Country, but Section 2146 of the statute provided that federal law would not apply to Indians who commit wrongs against other Indians of the same band who have been punished by the local law of the tribe. The Brule' tribal council convened with Crow Dog and the family of Spotted Tail and resolved the case according to tribal custom. The case was resolved in a civil manner through mediation and peacemaking. Restitution was the remedy provided by the parties and was consistent with tribal custom law. Crow Dog agreed to pay $600, eight horses and a blanket to the Spotted Tail family, which the Spotted Tail family agreed to accept. The case was closed as far as the Brule' band was concerned. It was the Agent and other officials who were alarmed that Crow Dog was not severely punished for his offense. They lobbied for federal prosecution of Crow Dog in the Territorial Court of the United States. The government accepted the case and Crow Dog's trial was held at Deadwood in Dakota Territory. The U.S. Attorney for Dakota Territory argued that the "bad man amongst the Indians" clause repealed the exemption found in Section 2146. The Dakota Territorial District Court agreed, and Crow Dog was tried and convicted of murder. His penalty was a death sentence. On appeal to the U.S. Supreme Court, however, the government's argument did not prevail. The high court overturned Crow Dog's conviction on grounds that Article 1 referred to victims who were subject to the authority of the United States, and not to the Lakota nation. The court also noted that the penalty for failure to deliver up the wrongdoer was punishable by a reduction in rations, which logically meant that the victim could not be of the same band. The Court upheld the sovereignty of the Lakota nation by noting that there was no federal law that imposed the authority of the United States on Indian nations who were governed by their own custom law. The federal court lacked criminal jurisdiction to prosecute Indians who commit crimes against Indians of the same band in Indian country.

The case for federal jurisdiction was taken to Congress. The Bureau of Indian Affairs, agents and officials lobbied Congress for a law that would impose federal jurisdiction over felonies committed by Indians on the reservations. Congress reacted, and in 1885 the Major Crimes Act was adopted. The Major Crimes Act applied to all Indian reservations throughout the United States. The federal law is the source of authority for the U.S. Marshalls to investigate felonies on the reservation and for the U.S. Attorney to prosecute the cases in federal court. Most Indians who serve time in prison are there due to federal prosecution of crimes committed on Indian reservations.

The Crow Dog case represents a severe clash of cultures. The Brule' band handled the intertribal matter according to the needs of the community. The band was the most important element in the lives of its members. Survival of the band was dependent on the cooperation and contributions of its members. Each member had a role in serving the community. If a hunter was successful in killing a buffalo, for example, the entire village, or tiospaye would benefit from his success. The women had their roles in butchering and cooking the meat for all to eat. They also were responsible for skinning and tanning of buffalo hides to make tipis, or lodges, clothing, and robes. An individual served the entire community, and remedies for offenses were those that benefited the community, and not just the relatives of an offended person. Crow Dog was essential to the Brule' band, and for that reason he was not banished from the community. The death penalty did not exist in the Lakota culture. If one individual was excessively harmful to the group, he would be banished. Banishment was more humane or civil in the Lakota communities. Cooperation was most essential because it contributed to the survival of the nation.

That aspect of Lakota culture was lost on government officials, who argued to Congress that "red man's revenge" would create family feuds, and that relatives of Spotted Tail would kill relatives of Crow Dog, that Crow Dog's relatives would retaliate and the result would be a blood bath on the reservation. The argument was simply not tenable, but there was no one to educate Congress on the peaceful and cooperative lifestyles of the Lakota communities. Generosity and Respect are two of the most important values of Lakota culture. Because of the closely-knit communities, no one individual became wealthy, and no one individual was impoverished. The community prospered or declined not as individuals, but as a group. Leaders were selected because of their bravery, wisdom, generosity, and respect they showed to members of the band. Leaders put the interest and well-being of the people first and foremost over their own.

Ironically, the whites labeled the plains Indians as "savages" and set out to exterminate or to assimilate them, depending on the conscience of those who were bent on affecting the lives of Native Americans. In the eyes of those whites who clamored for Crow Dog's death, it was more humane and civil to put Crow Dog to death rather than let him live and contribute to the welfare of the band. This raises the question: Who were the actual savages?

As a consequence, the sovereignty of the Indian nations was affected and continues to be affected today. The Major Crimes Act now includes a total of sixteen major crimes. 18 U.S.C.A. 1153 now reads:

"Any Indian who commits against the person or property of another Indian or other person any of the following offenses, namely, murder, manslaughter, kidnapping, maiming, rape, involuntary sodomy, carnal knowledge of any female, not his wife, who has not attained the age of sixteen years, assault with intent to commit rape, incest, assault resulting in serious bodily injury, arson, burglary, robbery, and a felony under section 661 of this title within the Indian country, shall be subject to the same law and penalties as all other persons committing any of the above offenses, within the exclusive jurisdiction of the United States. As used in this section, the offenses of burglary, involuntary sodomy, and incest shall be defined and punished in accordance with the laws of the State in which such offense was committed as are in force at the time of such offense. In addition to the offenses of burglary, involuntary sodomy, and incest, any other of the above offenses which are not defined and punished by Federal law in force within the exclusive jurisdiction of the United States shall be defined and punished in accordance with the laws of the State in which such offense was committed as are in force at the time of such offense."

The **"bad men among the whites"** clause in Article 1 was invoked recently in a case that was brought before the United States Court of Federal Claims. Lavetta Elk, a member of the Oglala Sioux Tribe sought relief under Article 1 of the treaty that provides that if bad men among the whites commit any wrong upon the person or property of any Sioux, the United States will reimburse the injured person for the loss sustained. The court found that Ms. Elk was entitled to a judgment against the United States in the amount of $590,755.06.

The facts established that in 2002 Lavetta Elk was a student at Red Cloud High School on the Pine Ridge Indian Reservation. She wished to join the U.S. Army and be the first female in her family to be in the military. She requested enlistment information from the recruiting office and a Staff Sergeant Joseph Kropf was the Army recruiter who was assigned to work with her from the Rapid City, South Dakota recruiting station. Kropf did much more than provide recruiting assistance. He began sending her flowers at the hospital where she worked, attended her volleyball games and showed much more than a personal interest in her life. Lavetta declined his invitations to attend social events such as movies repeatedly. Lavetta declined his personal advances toward her and eventually cut off communications. Her desire to enlist in the Army however was enough to convince her to reestablish communications with Kropf. Lavetta graduated from Red Cloud high School in May 2002. Kropf took her on a recruiting trip and he would grab her, hug her around the waist, and attempt to kiss her. She became angry and pushed him away, but Kopf would not stop the harassment even after apologizing for his behavior. Eventually, Lavetta escaped from Kopf's vehicle while on a trip through the reservation and she reported his behavior after one especially egregious incident where he actually attacked her while in the vehicle. She contacted an attorney and in April, 2004, she sent a Notice of Claim to the Department of the Interior which invoked both the Federal Tort Claims Act (FTCA) and the "bad men" clause of the 1868 Treaty. The Army denied the FTCA claim and Lavetta heard nothing about her complaint with the Interior Department. Several procedural motions were held and the Court denied the Interior Department's Motion to Dismiss in 2006. A full trial was held in the Court of Claims on April 28-30, 2008. The court found that Lavetta suffered emotional injuries, pain and suffering, economic damages, and lost opportunity to join the Army, including the training and career benefits to which she could have earned.

A literal reading of the "bad men" clause in the Fort Laramie Treaty of 1868 indicates that the clause would apply to all white men who turned out to be "bad'. For example, the soldiers of the Seventh Cavalry who massacred Big Foot's band on December 30, 1890, at Wounded Knee, would qualify as bad men among the whites. Big Foot and his people were not violating any law, they were present on the Pine Ridge Indian Reservation where they had a right to be; they had not committed any crimes and their behavior was peaceful. They were participants in the Ghost Dance, which was a spiritual rite involving prayer for the disappearance of the whites and a return of the buffalo. They were in fact, seeking sanctuary with the Oglala people at Pine Ridge. The killing of Big Foot, his men, and the women and children by the soldiers of the Seventh Cavalry was a "wrong upon the person or property of the Indians" and the soldiers should have been arrested and punished according to the laws of the United States, as the treaty says, and the injured Indians and surviving relatives should have been compensated for their injuries and losses. Instead the soldiers were decorated with medals of honor for showing bravery. They were considered "brave" for killing unarmed men, women, and children. This massacre is a disgrace to the United States, and it has left a permanent impression on Indians throughout the nation of the destruction and devastation that can be brought on by bad men among the whites and others who condone such actions. Indians today wonder who the real "savages" were throughout the history of this country.

In 1866, Ulysses S. Grant was promoted to the position of General of the Army. He later became the U.S. President, and in 1874, as President, he allowed the Army to ignore the gold miners who were trespassing into the Black Hills. This behavior would also qualify him as a "bad man among the whites", because it resulted in the loss of Indian property.

"Article 2—The United States agrees that the following district or country to wit, viz: commencing on the east bank of the Missouri River where the 46th parallel of north latitude crosses the same, thence along low-water mark down said east bank to a point opposite where the northern line of the State of Nebraska strikes the river, and along the northern line of Nebraska to the 104th parallel of north latitude intercepts the same, thence due east along said parallel to the place of the beginning in addition thereto, all existing reservations of the east back of said river, shall be and the same is, set apart for the absolute and undisturbed use and occupation of the Indians herein named, and for such other friendly tribes or individual Indians as from time to time they may be willing, with the consent of the United States, to admit amongst them; and the United States now solemnly agrees that no persons, except those herein designated and authorized so to do, and except such officers, agents, and employees of the government as may be authorized to enter upon Indian reservations in discharge of duties enjoined by law, shall ever be permitted to pass over, settle upon, or reside in the territory described in this article, or in such territory as may be added to this reservation for the use of said Indians and henceforth they will and do hereby relinquish all claims or right in and to any portion of the United States or territories, except such as is embraced within the limits aforesaid, and except as hereinafter provided."

Article 2 established the Great Sioux Reservation. The boundaries include all of South Dakota west of the Missouri River, the northern half of the State of Nebraska, all lands east of the Big Horn Mountains, a corner of Montana and approximately one fourth of the lands lying west of the Missouri River in North Dakota. (See Appendix D)

"Article 3—If it should appear from actual survey or other satisfactory examination of said tract of land that it contains less than one hundred and sixty acres of tillable land for each person who, at the time, may be authorized to reside on it under the provisions of this treaty, and a very considerable number of such persons shall be disposed to commence cultivating the soil as farmers, the United States agrees to set apart, for the use of said Indians, herein provided, such additional quantity of arable land, adjoining to said reservation, or as near to the same as it can be obtained, as may be required to provide the necessary amount."

While Article 3 purports to provide enough land so that every Indian would become assimilated into the farming culture of the United States, the history of the events prove that this article was never intended to provide additional land for the Lakota nation. The fact is that most of the land reserved in Article 2 was lost to white farmers which shows that Article 3 was but a feeble attempt to show good faith on the part of the United States.

"Article 4—The United States agrees, at its own proper expense, to construct, at some place on the Missouri river, near the center of said reservation where timber and water may be convenient, the following buildings, to wit: a warehouse, a storeroom for the use of the agent in storing goods belonging to the Indians, to cost not less than $2,500; an agency building, for the residence of the agent, to cost not exceeding $3,000, a residence for the physician, to cost not more than $3,000; and five other buildings for a carpenter, farmer, blacksmith, miller, and engineer—each to cost not exceeding $2,000; also a school-house, or mission building as soon as a sufficient number of children can be induced by the agent to attend school, which shall not cost exceeding $5,000. The United States agrees further to cause to be erected on said reservation near other buildings herein authorized, a good steam circular saw-mill, with a grist-mill and shingle machine attached to the same, to cost not exceeding $8,000."

In Article 4 the United States assumes the duty to construct buildings on the reservation to house its employees with the aim of assimilating Indians into mainstream America.

"**Article 5.—The United States agrees that the agent for said Indians shall in the future make his home at the agency building; that he shall reside among them, and keep an office open at all times for the purpose of prompt and diligent inquiry into such matters of complaint by and against the Indians as may be presented for investigation under the provisions of their treaty stipulations, and also for the faithful discharge of other duties enjoined on him by law in all cases of depredation on person or property he shall cause the evidence to be taken in writing and forwarded together with these findings, to the Commissioner of Indian Affairs, whose decision, subject to the revision of the Secretary of the Interior, shall be binding on the parties to this treaty.**"

The agent of the government assumed the role of arbitrator of disputes among Indians. Article 5 authorized the agent to reside at the agency building and conduct business with the Indians on behalf of the United States. Today, the local Agency Superintendent, handles only complaints made by Indians against Bureau of Indian Affairs employees, and supervises government employees and officials. He does not arbitrate complaints made by Indians against other Indians, and is not involved in controversies unless the matter involves land held in trust by the United States. As an agent of the United States, however, he is under a duty to protect the rights of all citizens within his jurisdiction and this can involve protection of civil rights of tribal members

---

"**Article 6—If any individual belonging to said tribes of Indians, or legally incorporated with them, being the head of a family, shall desire to commence farming, he shall have the privilege to select, in the presence and with the assistance of the agent then in charge, a tract of land within said reservation, not exceeding three hundred and twenty acres in extent, which tract, when so selected, certified, and recorded in the "Land Book" as herein directed, shall cease to be held in common, but the same may be occupied and held in the exclusive possession of the person selecting it, and of his family, so long as he or they may continue to cultivate it.**

Any person over eighteen years of age, not being the head of a family, may in like manner select and cause to be certified to him or her, for purposes of cultivation, a quantity of land, not exceeding eighty acres in extent, and thereupon be entitled to the exclusive possession of the same as above directed.

For each tract of land so selected, a certificate, containing a description thereof and the name of the person selecting it, with a certificate endorsed thereon that the same has been recorded, shall be delivered to the party entitled to it, by the agent, after the same shall have been recorded by him in a book to be kept in his office, subject to inspection, which said book shall be known as the "Sioux Land Book".

The President may, at any time, order a survey of the reservation, and, when so surveyed, Congress shall provide for protecting the rights of said settlers in their improvements, and may fix the character of the title held by each. The United States may pass such laws on the subject of alienation and descent of property between the Indians and their descendants as may be thought proper. And it is further stipulated that any male Indians over eighteen years of age, of any band or tribe that is or shall hereafter become a party to this treaty, who now is or who shall hereafter become a resident or occupant of any reservation or territory not included in the tract of country designated and described in this treaty for the permanent home of the Indians, which is not mineral land, nor reserved by the United States for special purposes other than Indian occupation, and who shall have made improvements thereon of the value of two hundred dollars or more, and continuously occupied the same as a homestead for the term of three years shall be entitled to receive from the United States a patent for one hundred and sixty acres of land including his said improvements, the same to be in the form of the legal subdivisions of the surveys of the public lands. Upon application in writing, sustained by the proof of two disinterested witnesses, made to the register of the local land office when the land sought to be entered is within a land district, application and proof being made to the Commissioner of the General Land Office, and the right of such Indian or Indians to enter such tract or tracts of land shall accrue and be perfect from the date of his first improvements thereon, and shall continue as long as he continues his residence and improvements and no longer. And any Indian or Indians receiving a patent for land under the foregoing provisions shall thereby and from thenceforth become and be a citizen of the United States and be entitled to all the privileges and immunities of such citizens, and shall, at the same time, retain all his rights to benefits accruing to Indians under this treaty."

Article 6 comprises classic misunderstandings that Raymond DeMallie found in his studies of treaties and their meanings. The provision that entitles an Indian who commences farming to select land, and receive a certificate with its description on file in the Sioux Land Book was beyond the experience of the Lakota people. The Lakota agreed to retain a large portion of their land in exchange for lands outside the boundaries of the Great Sioux Reservation to which they had a rightful claim. Lakota land was held in common with all members of the band. The idea of private ownership of land was contrary to the Lakota culture and their means of survival. Culturally, the land was held as sacred. *Unci Maka* (Grandmother Earth) was considered to be the mother of all natural beings, including man, animal, plant and spirits. One simply could not own a portion of Mother Earth. On the contrary, Mother Earth owns the Lakota people and all life that exists on her. To divide up the reservation and claim individual ownership to tracts of land was incomprehensible to the Lakota. It was clearly a ploy on the part of the United States to change the lifestyle of the Lakota people to the point of becoming U.S. citizens. The latter was not something that the Lakota people wanted or requested. It was inserted into the treaty without a proper explanation and was designed to benefit the United States rather than the Lakota people. Article 6 marks the beginning of a devastating cultural change in the lives of the Lakota people. It also provided a "legitimate" means for whites to acquire additional Indian land without having to comply with existing treaty law.

Article 6 of the treaty did not usher in a lot of Indians as U.S. citizens. Congress reacted in 1924 and enacted the Indian Citizenship Act, which declared all American Indians to be U.S. citizens.

"Article 7—In order to insure the civilization of the Indians entering into this treaty, the necessity of education is admitted, especially of such of them as are or may be settled on said agricultural reservations, and they, therefore, pledge themselves to compel their children, male and female, between the ages of six and sixteen years, to attend school, and it is hereby made the duty of the agent for said Indians to see that this stipulation is strictly complied with; and the United States agrees that for every thirty children between said ages, who can be induced or compelled to attend school, a house shall be provided, and a teacher competent to teach the elementary branches of an English education shall be furnished, who will reside among said Indians and faithfully discharge his or her duties as a teacher. The provisions of this article to continue for not less than twenty years."

Article 7 is the genesis of the Office of Indian Education. The education commitment has been extended far beyond the twenty years, and it has progressed beyond the elementary levels of education to high school, college and graduate school. In 1970, President Nixon announced the policy of self-determination and the implementing legislation has enabled Indian tribes to contract BIA schools and departments. Most reservation schools are now contract schools administered by local Indian school boards and staff. The requirement that the education be an "English" education has undermined the native languages and the reservation schools are now teaching Native Languages, History and Culture. Article 7 was also designed to serve the needs of the United States in its efforts to assimilate the Indians into mainstream American society.

"Article 8—When the head of a family or lodge shall have selected lands and received his certificate as above directed, and the agent shall be satisfied that he intends in good faith to commence cultivating the soil for a living, he shall be entitled to receive seeds and agricultural implements for the first year, not exceeding in value one hundred dollars, and for each succeeding year he shall continue to farm, for a period of three years more, he shall be entitled to receive seeds and implements as aforesaid, not exceeding in value twenty-five dollars. And it is further stipulated that such persons as commence farming shall receive instruction from the farmer herein provided for and whenever more than one hundred persons shall enter upon the cultivation of the soil, a second blacksmith shall be provided with such iron, steel, and other material as may be needed."

The government provided "boss farmers" to the reservation districts during the early part of the twentieth century. Many Indian families were provided with wagons, harnesses, mowing machines, rakes, and other tools for farming and ranching. A vast majority of Indians did not take to farming and ranching. It simply was not in their life experiences. Several families did take up the new economic activity and continue to do so. The Bureau of Indian Affairs continues to manage most of the land that was eventually allotted to Indians as long as the land remains in trust. Most allotments are held in leasing units and the land is used by both Indian and white ranchers and farmers. The most valuable acreage was opened to white settlers under the General Allotment Act of 1887, wherein the government declared such land to be "unalloted surplus land", implying that the land was no longer needed by the Indians.

"Article 9—At any time after ten years from the making of this treaty, the United States shall have the privilege of withdrawing the physician, farmer, blacksmith, carpenter, engineer, and miller herein provide for, but in case of such withdrawal, an additional sum thereafter of ten thousand dollars per annum shall be devoted

to the education of said Indians, and the Commissioner of Indian Affairs, shall upon careful inquiry into their condition, make such rules and regulations for the expenditure of said sums as will best promote the education and moral improvement of said tribes."

The government continues to provide medical personnel to the reservations. The provision of health services, including hospitals, clinics, physicians, nurses and other personnel are contingent upon funding by the Indian Health Service. There is a shortage of medical personnel and funding available to Indians and many Indians must rely on Veterans Administration services if they are veterans. Others rely on Medicaid, Medicare, or insurance.

"Article 10—In lieu of all sums of money or other annuities provided to be paid to the Indians herein named under any treaty or treaties heretofore made, the United States agrees to deliver at the agency house on the reservation herein named, on or before the first day of August of each year, for thirty years, the following articles, to wit:

For each male person over 14 years of age, a suit of good substantial woolen clothing consisting of coat, pantaloons, flannel shirt, hat, and a pair of home-made socks.

For each female over 12 years of age, a flannel shirt, or the goods necessary to make it, a pair of woolen hose, 12 yards of calico, and 12 yards of cotton domestics.

For the boys and girls under the ages named, such flannel and cotton goods as may be needed to make each a suit as aforesaid, together with a pair of woolen hose for each.

And in order that the Commissioner of Indian Affairs may be able to estimate properly for the articles herein named, it shall be the duty of the agent each year to forward to him a full and exact census of the Indians, on which the estimate from year to year can be based.

And in addition to the clothing herein named, the sum of $10 for each person entitled to the beneficial effects of this treaty shall be annually appropriated for a period of 30 years, while such persons roam and hunt, and $20 for each person who engaged

in farming, to be used by the Secretary of the Interior in the purchase of such articles as from time to time the condition and necessities of the Indians may indicate to be proper. And if within the 30 years, at any time, it shall appear that the amount of money needed for clothing, under this article, can be appropriated to better uses for the Indians named herein, Congress may, by law, change the appropriation to other purposes, but in no event shall the amount of the appropriation be withdrawn or discontinued for the period named. And the President shall annually detail an officer of the Army to be present and attest the delivery of all the goods herein named, to the Indians, and he shall inspect and report on the quantity and quality of the goods and the manner of their delivery. And it is hereby expressly stipulated that each Indian over the age of four years, who shall have removed to and settled permanently upon said reservation, one pound of meat and one pound of flour per day, provided the Indians cannot furnish their own subsistence at an earlier date. And it is further stipulated that the United States will furnish and deliver to each lodge of Indians or family of persons legally incorporated with them, who shall remove to the reservation herein described and commence farming, one good American cow, and one good well-broken pair of American oxen within 60 days after such lodge or family shall have so settled upon said reservation."

By 1868 most of the buffalo had been killed off by fur traders, emigrants and forty-niners. The buffalo had not only been killed off; most were scattered about the country, and they had also decimated the grasslands, which supported the buffalo. Miners killed buffalo recklessly for sport or their hides, and the meat was left on the plains to rot. Wolves, coyotes and other animal predators must have feasted lavishly on the carcasses of dead buffalos. The white man's gain was the Indians' loss.

With the demise of the buffalo, the Lakota could not sustain themselves. The buffalo provided all the necessities of food, shelter and clothing. The government was aware of this and Article 10 attempts to address the needs for clothing and the goods necessary to make the clothing. This, too, was a drastic change in the lifestyle of the Lakota. Not only was their diet affected, but also their clothing and housing needs.

Article 10 also reflects the government's wish for the Indians to reject their roaming and hunting ways and to adopt a farming culture. Monetary inducements were used to persuade Indians to give up their old ways of life and to adopt the so-called civilized, sedentary lifestyle.

"Article 11—In consideration of the advantages and benefits conferred by this treaty and the many pledges of friendship by the United States, the tribes who are parties to this agreement hereby stipulate that they will relinquish all right to occupy permanently the territory outside their reservations as herein defined, but yet reserve the right to hunt on any lands north of North Platte, and on the Republican Fork of the Smoky Hill river, so long as the buffalo may range thereon in such numbers as to justify the chase. And they, the said Indians further express agree:

1st. That they will withdraw all opposition to the construction of the railroads now being built on the plains.

2nd. That they will permit the peaceful construction of any railroad not passing over their reservation as herein defined.

3d. That they will not attack any persons at home, or traveling, nor molest or disturb any wagon trains, coaches, mules, or cattle belonging to the people of the United States, or to persons friendly therewith.

4th. They will never capture, or carry off from the settlements, white women or children.

5th. They will never kill or scalp white men, nor attempt to do them harm.

6th. They withdraw all pretence of opposition to the construction of the railroad now being built along the Platte river and westward to the Pacific ocean, and they will not in future object to the construction of railroads, wagon roads, mail stations, or other works of utility or necessity, which may be ordered or permitted by the laws of the United States. But should such roads or other works be constructed on the lands of their reservation, the government will pay the tribe whatever amount of damage may be assessed by three disinterested commissioners to be appointed by the President for that purpose one of the said commissioners to be a chief or headman of the tribe.

7th. They agree to withdraw all opposition to the military posts or roads now established south of the North Platte river, or that may be established, not in violation of treaties heretofore made or hereafter to be made with any of the Indian tribes."

"The railroads" referred to those being built around the Great Sioux Reservation, particularly south of the North Platte River, which was outside the boundaries of the reservation. The Lakota agreed not to harm white women and children. Such a pledge, however, was not necessary. There were probably isolated instances where women and children were taken into the camps, but it was not customary for the warriors to attack and kill women and children. That was limited to the white soldiers. It was common for them to destroy an Indian village, burn the lodges, burn their supplies, kill their ponies and kill every Indian they could regardless of age or sex. For example, in 1855, Colonel William Harney unleashed his troops and canons on Iron Shell's Brule' camp and Little Thunder's Oglala camp at Ash Hollow. Over eighty Indians were killed, many of them women and children. About seventy women and children, though wounded, were taken to Fort Laramie and held as hostages. Chief Spotted Tail, Long Chin, and Red Leaf surrendered themselves up and agreed to be held at Fort Leavenworth in exchange for the release of the women and children.

Wounded Knee is another example of the barbarous attacks on women and children by white soldiers. Medals of honor are usually bestowed on those who save lives, but in the Wounded Knee Massacre, the soldiers were honored for destroying innocent lives.

The Sand Creek Massacre occurred in November 1864, when Colonel John Chivington and his gang of 600 volunteers slaughtered 200 peaceful Southern Cheyenne and Arapahos, two thirds of them were unarmed elders, women and children. Colonel Chivington himself was a former Methodist preacher. When asked about the killing of Indian babies he replied, "nits make lice". (BHWJ p. 29) Nothing was left of Black Kettle's camp; their lodges were burned, their ponies were killed and their food supplies were burned. Those women and children who escaped the initial onslaught were hunted down and murdered. Their scalps and pubic hair was cut out and taken as souvenirs. Ironically, Black Kettle's Cheyenne and White Antelope's Arapaho were camped at Sand Creek because the government promised them that Sand Creek would be a safe place for them to camp. The attitude of Colonel Chivington was typical of Indian-haters of the times. John Chivington, who professed to be a Methodist preacher, ignored the teachings of Christ, which include love, compassion, humility, and peace. To Lakota Christians, Chivington was the living definition of the anti-Christ, because he performed the work of the devil. After the massacre, the Cheyenne and the Arapaho nations became allies of the Sioux in their efforts to defend themselves and their lands.

Simply put, Article 11 is a promise by the Lakota that they will not engage in the same kind of atrocities as the white soldiers. It was a very easy concession for the Lakota to make because cruelty to women and children contradicted the habits and customs of the Lakota; the same conditions and promises should have been directed to the United States as well.

"Article 12—No treaty for the cession of any portion or part of the reservation herein described which may be held in common, shall be of any validity or force as against the said Indians unless executed and signed by at least three-fourths of all the adult male Indians occupying or interested in the same, and no cession by the tribe shall be understood or construed in such manner as to deprive, without his consent, any individual member of the tribe of his rights to any tract of land selected by him as provided in Article 6 of this treaty"

Article 12 has proven to be the most important aspect of the treaty in terms of litigation, politics, and tribal concern; particularly the Black Hills, which Congress removed from the Great Sioux Reservation through legislation on February 28, 1877.

In 1848 Father Peter John DeSmet visited with the Lakota in the Black Hills. A chief offered him a bag of "glimmering powder" which the priest recognized as gold. He immediately warned the chief, "Put it away and show it to nobody." (South Dakota, p.42] Word eventually spread that there was gold in the Black Hills and in no time thousands of whites were swarming the Black Hills in search of the valuable mineral.

The same problem which led to the creation and violation of the 1851 Fort Laramie Treaty led to violation of the 1868 Fort Laramie Treaty—the discovery of gold, this time in the Black Hills which had been reserved to the Sioux in the Fort Laramie Treaty. In 1874, the U.S. Army undertook an exploratory expedition into the Black Hills under the command of Lieutenant Colonel George Armstrong Custer. Custer, his 1,000 soldiers, teamsters and aids left Fort Abraham Lincoln located in North Dakota on the Missouri River. They left on July 2, 1874. They reached the Black Hills in late July 1874, and confirmed the presence of gold in the area. Custer's description of the hills, the gold, the landscape, the beautiful pine clad hills, and the abundance of water, grasses and, timber instigated a public demand for the opening of the Hills for white settlement. The Bismarck Tribune described the hills as "One of the most beautiful spots on God's green earth; no wonder the Indians regard this as the home of the Great Spirit and guard it with jealous care." (BHWJ p. 75)

After Custer returned to Fort Abraham Lincoln, he publicly reported the richness of the Black Hills. One of his writings stated that he had "found gold in the roots of the grass at an expense of but little time or labor." News of Custer's findings prompted thousands of more men to begin preparations for invading the Hills.

President Ulysses S Grant initially sought to honor the treaty by ordering the Army to keep the miners out of the Black Hills. On September 3, 1874, the Army warned the public that it would "burn the wagons and destroy the outfit and arrest the leaders" of mining groups who attempted to move into the Black Hills. The miners who had infested the Hills by the spring of 1875 ignored the warning. President Grant concluded that the acquisition of the Hills was inevitable. The Army's efforts to curb the influx of miners into the Hills were futile. A most troubling aspect regarding the trespassing of gold miners into the Hills was the fact that the United States knew of the infractions, but decided not to enforce its solemn treaty commitments. President Grant secretly ordered Brigadier General A. H. Terry to ignore a previous order for the miners to stay out of the Black Hills. On November 9, 1875, General Phillip H. Sheridan wrote a letter to General Terry describing a meeting which occurred in Washington on November 3, 1875, between the President, the Secretary of the Interior, the Secretary of War and General Sheridan wherein he writes: ". . . **the President decided that while the orders heretofore issued forbidding the occupation of the Black Hills country, by miners, should not be rescinded, still no further resistance by the military should be made to the miners going in: it being his belief that such resistance only increased their desire and complicated the troubles. Will you therefore quietly cause the troops in your Department to assume such attitudes as will meet the views of the President in this respect." (Signed) P. H. Sheridan, Lieut. General."**

On November 3, 1875, President Grant made the following statement to General Crook and General Sheridan that "**no further resistance shall be made to miners going into the Black Hills.**" General Sherman wrote to one of his subordinate officers, that if miners wished to invade the Black Hills, "**I understand that the President and the Interior Department will wink at it.**" (BHWJ p. 83)

The Government responded to public demands to acquire the Black Hills by appointing a commission headed by William B. Allison to negotiate a purchase of the Black Hills from the Sioux. Negotiations for the sale of the Hills were unsuccessful. The Commission offered the Indians an annual rental of $400,000, or a payment of $6 million for total relinquishment of the Hills. The Sioux demanded at least $70 million and negotiations broke down.

In the winter of 1875-76, while the Lakota were lawfully hunting in Indian country in accordance with the treaty, the Army was dispatched to confront the Lakota who did not favor the treaty and decided that they would be considered "hostiles". The agents were advised that all Lakota must report to the agencies by January 31, 1876, or be declared "hostile", a designation which meant that any Lakota could be shot on sight by any soldier. The word was given on December 6, 1875 and did not reach those hunters who were out hunting in those areas that were approved by the treaty. Nevertheless, on February 1, 1876, the Secretary of the Interior relinquished jurisdiction over all "hostiles" to the Army. Custer's campaign against the so-called "hostiles" led to his defeat at the Battle of the Little Big Horn on June 25, 1876.

Following the Battle of the Little Big Horn, Congress imposed a strict "sell or starve" ultimatum to the Lakota. The buffalo were gone, and the Sioux could not sustain themselves without the rations that were promised in the treaties. The government promised that there would be no rations at all unless the Sioux agreed to sell the Black Hills to the United States. The commission, headed by George Manypenny, presented a treaty in which the Sioux would relinquish all rights to the Black Hills and lands west of the Black Hills as far as the Rocky Mountains. In addition, lands north and south of the Black Hills would be relinquished to the United States in exchange for subsistence rations for as long as they would be needed to ensure the Sioux survival. According to Article 12 of the Fort Laramie Treaty of 1868, "No treaty for the cession of any portion or part of the reservation . . . shall be of any validity or force against the said Indians unless executed and signed by at least three-fourths of all the adult male Indians occupying or interested in the same . . ."

The commission was able to obtain signatures of only ten percent of all adult male Indians. Congress, nevertheless, enacted the agreement into law as the Act of Feb. 28, 1877, 19 Stat. 254, thereby taking the Black Hills from the Great Sioux Reservation and appropriating it into the public domain.

The Act of February 28, 1877, is clearly a breach of Article 12. Not only in the unlawful taking of the land, but the manner in which it was done. The reference to "bad men among the whites" in Article 1 of the treaty applied to thousands of miners in the Black Hills, the soldiers who failed to keep them out, and most outrageously, the President of the Unite States. President Grant's actions were unconscionable. He could have been legally arrested and punished according to the laws of the United States for his actions as a bad man among the whites. And the Indians could have, and should have, been reimbursed for the loss of resources in the Black Hills. Article 6 of the U. S. Constitution provides that the Constitution, Laws, and Treaties of the United States are the supreme law of the land. On November 3, 1875, there was no federal law in place that superseded the Treaty. The Treaty was the supreme law of the land, and the President as well as his officers were all sworn to uphold the Constitution in the performance of their duties. The Treaty has a remedy written into Article l, which provides that if a bad white man who shall commit any wrong upon the person or property of the Indians, the United States will, upon proof made to the agent, and forwarded to the Commissioner of Indian Affairs at Washington city, proceed at once to cause the offender to be arrested and punished according to the laws of the United States, and also reimburse the injured person for the loss sustained. President Grant and his aides could have, and should have, been arrested and punished according to the laws of the United States.

Article 12 was also violated in 1910 when Congress diminished the Pine Ridge Indian Reservation by removing Bennett County from the reservation without the consent of 3/4ths of all adult male Indians. This case is related to the General Allotment Act of 1887, which is discussed in a later chapter.

"Article 13—The United Sates hereby agrees to furnish annually to the Indians the physician, teachers, carpenter, miller, engineer, farmer, and blacksmiths, as herein contemplated, and that such appropriations shall be made from time to time, on the estimate of the Secretary of the Interior, as will be sufficient to employ such persons."

Physicians and teachers sufficient to serve the needs of the people have never been provided. A shortage of physicians continues to exist on the reservations because the Government treats the Indian Health Service as another division of the Health and Humans Services Department, instead of a nation entitled to medical services through the treaty.

"Article 14—It is agreed that the sum of five hundred dollars annually for three years from date shall be expended in presents for the ten persons of said tribe who in the judgment of the agent may grow the most valuable crops for the respective year."

Article 14 is aimed at assimilating the Indians into the farming culture by rewarding the ten most productive farmers for three years after the signing of the treaty.

"Article 15—The Indians herein named agree that when the agency house and other buildings shall be constructed on the reservation named, they will regard said reservation their permanent home, and they will make no permanent settlement elsewhere; but they shall have the right subject to the conditions and modifications of this treaty, to hunt, as stipulated in Article 11 hereof."

Article 15 attempts to restrict Indians to the reservation, which was acceptable to the Indians at the time. The reservations are considered to be the permanent home of most Lakota people although many have made their homes in communities off the reservation. In fact, a restriction keeping non-Indian U.S. citizens off the reservation should have been imposed. The right to hunt buffalo as long as the numbers justify the chase is meaningless today.

"Article 16—The United States hereby agrees and stipulates that the country north of the North Platte river and east of the summits of the Big Horn mountains shall be held and considered to be unceded Indian territory, and also stipulates and agrees that no white person or persons shall be permitted to settle upon or occupy any portion of the same; or without the consent of the Indians, first had and obtained, to pass through the same; and it is further agreed by the United States, that within ninety days after the conclusion of peace with all the bands of the Sioux nation, the military posts now established in the territory in this article named shall be abandoned, and that the road leading to them and by them to the settlements in the Territory of Montana shall be closed."

Article 16 addresses the Powder River country in Wyoming. It was designated as unceded Indian Territory, which meant that it remained within the Great Sioux Reservation, and that it was exclusively Indian Territory. The road leading to the settlements in Montana was the Bozeman Trail. Red Cloud insisted that the Bozeman Trail be closed and that the forts along the Bozeman Trail, which had been established for the protection of trespassers, be abandoned. Red Cloud held out for the concessions in Article 16 and was the last to sign the treaty. Shortly after the treaty was signed, Lakota warriors burned down the forts.

"Article 17—It is hereby expressly understood and agreed by and between the respective parties to the treaty that the execution of this treaty and its ratification by the United States Senate shall have the effect, and shall be construed as abrogating and annulling all treaties and agreements heretofore entered into between the respective parties hereto, so far as such treaties and agreements obligate the United States to furnish and provide money, clothing, or other articles of property to such Indians and bands of Indians as become parties to this treaty, but no further.

In testimony of all which, we, the said commissioners, and we, the chiefs and headmen of the Brule band of the Sioux Nation, have hereunto set our hands and seals at Fort Laramie, Dakota Territory, this twenty-ninth day of April, in the year one thousand eight hundred and sixty-eight."

N. G TAYLOR,

W. T. SHERMAN
Lieutenant General

WM. S. Harney
Brevet Major General U.S.A.

JOHN B. SANBORN,

S. F. TAPPAN

C. C AUGUR
Brevet Major General

ALFRED H. TERRY
Brevet Major General U. S. A.

Attest:

A. S H. WHITE, Secretary.

Article 17 abrogates all previous treaties signed by the United States and the various bands of the Lakota Nation insofar as obligating the United States to provide money and property. The Fort Laramie Treaty of 1851 provided that "the Indian nations do not hereby abandon or prejudice any rights or claims they may have to other lands; and further that they do not surrender the privilege of hunting, fishing or passing over any of the tracts of country heretofore described." Article 17 did not give up this portion of the 1851 treaty because it does not refer to money or property to be provided by the United States.

The remaining portion of the 1868 Fort Laramie Treaty consists of dates and signatures of Lakota men of different bands who signed on April 29, May 25, May 26 and November 6, 1869. (See Appendix B)

CHAPTER FIVE

THE GENERAL ALLOTMENT ACT OF 1887

The General Allotment Act was designed to accomplish two purposes: divide the reservations up into parcels of land that would be privately held by some of the Indians, and to allow whites to acquire more land from the Indians. This time it was reservation land established by the treaties that the Government would allow whites to invade.

The idea of allowing individual Indian ownership of the land had the support of everyone but the Indians. A member of Congress speaking on the Dawes Bill in 1886 said, "It has . . . the endorsement of the Indian rights associations throughout the country and of the best sentiment of the land" . . . (D.S. Otis HISTORY OF THE ALLOTMENT POLICY HEARINGS ON HR 7902 BEFORE THE HOUSE COMM. ON INDIAN AFFAIRS.)

Congress was not interested in how the Lakota would view the allotment policy. First of all, regarding the concept of property ownership, the Lakota culture was diametrically opposed to that of the whites. The whites did not understand the Native people's relationship to the earth. Native people believed in a communal system of property ownership, while the white immigrants believed in private or individual ownership. The Natives believed that the people belonged to "Unci Maka"—Grandmother Earth, and that no individual could own the Earth. Native people lived not to control or exploit the earth, but to live in harmony with nature. They considered themselves to be a part of the natural order of all living things, together with the four-legged, the plant life, the crawling insect life, the flying, and all forms of natural life. Wakan Tanka (Great Spirit), created all living things and the Lakota holds all forms of life to be spiritual and sacred. In traditional Lakota spirituality and belief, Wakan Tanka does not take on a personality, but is manifested in the sun, moon, sky, earth, winds, lightning, thunder and other natural phenomena. (Oglala Religion—William K. Powers p 45) The whites, on the other hand, viewed the earth as a thing to be exploited and owned. The wild beasts were to be exterminated so that room could be made for domestic animals. The basic philosophical differences between the whites and the Indians resulted in a destruction of Indian land and a vital part of Indian culture.

The basic provisions of the General Allotment Act were:

1. **A grant of 160 acres to each family head, and 80 acres to each single person over the age of 18 years as well as each orphan under the age of 18 years. A grant of 40 acres would be made to each single person under eighteen.**
2. **A patent in fee to be issued to every allottee, which would be held in trust by the Government for 25 years, during which time the land could not be alienated or encumbered.**
3. **A period of 4 years to be allowed for each Indian to select an allotment. Failure of the Indians to do so would result in a selection being made for them at the order of the Secretary of the Interior.**
4. **Citizenship to be conferred upon allottees and other Indians who had abandoned their tribes and adopted "the habits of civilized life".**

Because the Indian worldview differed so markedly from that of the white man, the whites assumed that their way of life was superior and that the Indian way of life was inferior, pagan, savage and uncivilized. The Agent for the Yankton Sioux wrote in 1877:

"As long as Indians live in villages they will retain many of their old and injurious habits. Frequent feasts, community in food, heathen ceremonies, and dances, constant visiting—these will continue as long as the people live together in close neighborhoods and villages . . . I trust that before another year is ended they will generally be located upon individual lands or farms. From that date will begin their real and permanent progress." These beliefs convinced Congress to unilaterally enact the Allotment Act what was ostensibly intended to benefit the Indians.

The provisions of the Dawes Allotment Act were very misleading and deceptive. First of all, not all Indians were granted allotments between the years, 1887 until 1934 when the allotment policy was terminated. Secondly, the law provided that Congress would offer so-called "unalloted surplus land" on the reservation to white settlers. The term, "Surplus land ", was a fiction. It was simply a means of opening Indian reservations to white settlers who were allowed to purchase so-called "surplus" land from the Government. Once the land was purchased and conveyed to the homesteader it would lose its "Indian land" status and would no longer be held in trust by the United States. The land would be classified as "deeded" land, which meant that it was no longer reservation land and the reservation would lose a part of its character. As a result, Indian reservations were greatly diminished in size, and the tribe would lose certain aspects of its sovereignty—jurisdiction. Additionally, the state is allowed to assess property taxes on reservation-deeded land.

Not every congressman was in favor of the Allotment Act. In 1881, Senator Teller stated:

"If I stand alone in the Senate, I want to put upon the record my prophesy in this matter, that when thirty or forty years shall have passed and these Indians shall have parted with title, they will curse the hand that was raised professedly in their defense to secure this kind of legislation, and if the people who are clamoring for it understood Indian character and Indian laws and Indian morals and Indian religion, they would not be here clamoring for this at all."

Unfortunately, Senator Teller was in the minority. A year earlier, the minority report of the House Indian Affairs reported that:

"The real aim of this bill is to get at the Indian lands and open them up to settlement. The provisions for this apparent benefit of the Indian are but a pretext to get at his lands and occupy them . . . If this were done in the name of greed, it would be bad enough, but to do it in the name of humanity, and under the cloak of an ardent desire to promote the Indian's welfare by making him like ourselves whether he will or not is infinitely worse."

Senator Teller and the House Minority Affairs Committee were right. The majority in Congress apparently heeded the message that President Gates of Amherst College when he spoke about teaching greed to the Indians:

"We have to begin with the absolute need of awakening in the savage broader desires and ampler wants. To bring him out of savagery into citizenship we must make the Indian more intelligently selfish before we can make him unselfishly intelligent. We need to awaken in him wants. In his dull savagery he must be touched by the wings of the divine angel of discontent. Then he begins to look forward, to reach out. The desire for property of his own may become an intense educating force. The wish for a home of his own awakens him to new efforts. Discontent with the tepee and the starving rations of the Indian camp in winter is needed to get the Indian out of the blanket and into trousers—and trousers with a pocket that aches to be filled with dollars . . . the truth is that there can be no strongly developed personality without the teaching of property, material property, and property in thoughts and convictions that are one's own. By acquiring property, man puts forth his personality and lays hold of matters by his own thought and will. Property has been defined as "objectified will". We all go to school to property if we use it wisely. No one has the right to the luxury of giving away, until he has learned the luxury of earning and possessing. The Saviors' teaching is full of illustrations of the right use of property . . . There is an intense moral training that comes from the use of property. And the Indian has had all that to learn." "Lake Mohonk Conference Proceedings, 189, 189 lg pg—11-12)

President Gates obviously knew nothing about Indian culture, Indian values, Indian spirituality or Indian life. His assumption that greed would contribute to the prosperity of the Indian people was seriously flawed. Greed was not acceptable to the Lakota people. Greed was contradictory to the Lakota value of generosity and respect. Lakota communities existed and survived because they lived in harmony with nature and did not thrive on material wealth. Greed was imposed on the Indians by the whites, who mixed greed with racism to legally steal millions of acres of treaty-protected Indian land.

National Impact of the Allotment Policy on Indian Land

In 1934 John Collier reported that: "The individualized parcels of allotted land have been held under Government trust over longer or shorter periods. Sometimes, where the land was agricultural, the Indian family has lived upon and has used one or more of the allotments attached to its several members. Where the land was of grazing character, or was timberland, allotment precluded the integrated use of the land by individuals or families, even at the start . . . Upon the Allottees death, it has been necessary to partition the land equally among heirs, or to sell it, and in the interim it has been leased. Most of the land of the living allottees has been leased to whites."

Through sales by the Government of the fictitiously designated "surplus" lands, sales by allottees after the trust period had ended or had been terminated by administrative action, and through sales by the Government of Indian heirship land, virtually mandatory under the Allotment Act, Indian land holdings was reduced from 138,000,000 acres in 1887 to 48,000,000 acres in 1934.

These gross statistics however are misleading, for of the remaining 48,000,000 acres, more than 20,000,000 are contained within areas that for special reasons have been exempted from the allotment law. Much of the remaining lands are comprised of badlands and lands that are not suitable for grazing or farming.

Most of the allotted lands that have been lost are the most valuable parts. Of the residual lands, taking all Indian-owned lands into account, nearly one-half, or nearly 20,000,000 acres are desert or semi desert lands. The loss of ninety million acres of land occurred after the treaty period ended in 1871. The Great Sioux Reservation established in 1868 consisted of 60,000,000 acres. The Act of February 28, 1877 reduced the Great

Sioux Reservation to slightly less than 22,000,000 acres. The Sioux Act of 1888 further reduced the Great Sioux Reservation to approximately 11,000,000 acres. The Great Sioux Reservation was abolished and five separate Indian reservations west of the Missouri River were established: Pine Ridge, Rosebud, Cheyenne River Lower Brule and Standing Rock. As the General Allotment Act was applied to the reservations, additional land was lost to white settlers. Consequently, the 11,000,000 acres is an overestimate. The total land base of the west river tribes amounts to much less than eleven million acres from the original sixty million acres. All of this land was lost not through treaties, but through the application of the allotment act. Thus, of the 90 million acres of Indian land lost through the allotment policy, Sioux land accounts for about 75 million acres that were lost.

Although the U.S. Constitution, Congressional Acts and U.S. Treaties designate Native Americans as Indian **Tribes**, that designation was not ascribed to the Lakota bands until 1889 when South Dakota became a state. The Great Teton Sioux Nation was reduced to five West River Lakota "Tribes". The bands were divided into separate tribes, each with their own government, their own constitution, and membership. The Government now deals with each tribe separately. When the U.S. Supreme Court renders a decision affecting one tribe, the decision applies to all tribes as though all tribes are one tribe.

The proverbial "divide and conquer" tactic has apparently worked for the Government, as it reduced the Lakota Nation and the Great Sioux Reservation to several tribes with a fraction of the land they held under a United States Treaty, which is supposed to be the "supreme law of the land" according Article 6 of the U.S. Constitution.

The Lakota bands of western South Dakota compose the Teton Lakota Sioux nation. There are presently five South Dakota Indian tribes occupying territory west of the Missouri River—the Oglala Sioux tribe at Pine Ridge, the Rosebud Sioux Tribe at Rosebud, the Lower Brule Sioux Tribe at Lower Brule, the Cheyenne River Sioux Tribe at Eagle Butte and the Standing Rock Sioux Tribe at Fort Yates, North Dakota. The groups were originally bands of the one Teton Lakota Nation sometimes referred to as the Teton Sioux which is comprise of the Oglala "Scatter their own", Sicangu "Burnt Thighs" Hunkpapa, "Those who camp at the end", Oohenumpa, "Two Kettles or Two Boilings", Itacipco "Without Bows—Sans Arc "(French name for "Without Bows") the Sihasapa, "Blackfeet", and the Minniconjou, "Planters by the Stream." The Cheyenne River Sioux Tribe is a mixture of Two Boilings, Without Bows, Blackfeet and Minniconjou. Each of these five reservations are made up of tribal land, individually owned Indian land, and white-owned deeded land. The Indian land is held in trust by the Government and is not taxable by the State Revenue Departments. The states do impose property taxes on white owned reservation land and deeded land owned by Indians—that is, land no longer held in trust by the Government.

Bennett County

Bennett County, South Dakota, lies in the southeastern part of the Pine Ridge Reservation. The General Allotment Act of 1887 was followed by several Homestead laws, which allowed white settlers to settle on Indian reservations. In1903 Congressman Burke introduced a bill to open 600,000 acres on the Rosebud Reservation at $4.00 per acre. The amount was reduced to 2500 claims totaling 400,000 acres. President Theodore Roosevelt signed the bill. (Dakota Indian Treaties p. 249)

The Sioux Falls Press reported:

"The white people need the land and the Indians are making no good use of them and would be infinitely better off without them. The Cheyenne River Reservation is ripe for opening and the Indians residing there-on are in good shape to take the lands in severalty and assume the ways and adopt the pursuit of civilization." *Ibid. 250*

In 1908 Tripp County on the Rosebud Reservation was opened to for white settlement. There were 114,780 registrations for the drawing of about 4,000 homesteads.

In 1909 the Standing Rock and Cheyenne River Indian reservations were opened to Homesteaders. Records from Kingsbury History stated: "There was a general and pronounced demand that all Indians in the state should be given allotments and the remainder of land left over on the reservations should be thrown open to settlement by whites. In short order this demand was actually carried into effect. There were 10,000 Homesteads thrown into the market." *Ibid p. 250.*

In February 1910, 1,400,000 acres in Pine Ridge and Rosebud reservations were ordered open for settlement. The bill passed Congress and the land became open for settlement by Proclamation of the President. 53,338 persons registered and the homesteads were taken by 1912, *Ibid.* p. 250

Cook v. Parkinson, United States Court of Appeals, Eighth Circuit, No 75-1306 (1975)

In 1971, a California Indian by the name of Donald M. Cook was arrested, charged and convicted for the crime of burglary in the town of Martin, SD. Martin is the county seat of Bennett County. He challenged the jurisdiction of South Dakota claiming that he is an Indian and that the crime was committed in Indian country.

The trial court denied his motion to dismiss, and in response he petitioned the U. S. District Court on a writ of habeas corpus. The U.S. District Court discharged the writ, ruling that the State of South Dakota does have jurisdiction in Bennett County. On appeal to the Eighth Circuit Court of Appeals, the higher court agreed with the District Court. The Court found that Bennett County was originally within the exterior boundaries of the Pine Ridge reservation. The Court stated, "Nevertheless, pursuant to the Act of 1910, Bennett County was not only opened to settlement but in our view was removed by cession from the Pine Ridge Indian Reservation." The Court referred to other cases involving the same issue around the same time. In the case, *Rosebud Sioux Tribe v. Kneip*, the issue was whether the Acts of April 23, 1904, March 2, 1907 and May 30, 1910 removed all or parts of Gregory, Tripp, Lyman, and Mellette Counties in South Dakota from the Rosebud Reservation as defined in the Act of March 2, 1889. In all these cases the federal courts found that the lands in question were severed from the Rosebud Reservation. The Court interpreted the reference to "the tract to be ceded" to mean that the land was actually removed from the reservation, and that the lands were no longer within the boundaries of the reservation. In the 1910 Act, the Act referred to Indians holding allotments in Bennett County and stated that "Provided that any Indian to whom allotments have been made on the tract to be ceded may, in case they elect to do so before such lands are offered for sale, relinquish same and select allotments in lieu thereof on the *diminished* reservation." The Court reasoned that the language in the law indicated Congress' intent to diminish the reservation instead of merely "opening" the reservation to white settlers. There was no mention of Article 12 of the Fort Laramie Treaty, which requires the consent of three-fourths of all male Indians before any sale of Indian land would be valid. At least one commissioner remarked that the Supreme Court ruled that Article 12 pursuant to the *Lone Wolf v. Hitchcock* case did not bind the United States. Actually, the Supreme Court did not take that position at all. It did say that the Tribes should go to Congress for relief when their land was unlawfully taken, and that the federal courts lacked jurisdiction to hear the matter without the consent of Congress.

The *Cook v. Parkinson* Court went on to say that South Dakota has jurisdiction over all deeded land in Bennett County because Bennett County is not on the reservation, and that the tribe and/or the federal government would have jurisdiction over Indians who commit crimes on trust lands within Bennett County.

The Act of May 27, 1910, and the impact of the law that authorized the sale of Indian land in Bennett County have created a jurisdictional maze. An Indian committing a crime in Bennett County may be subject to three judicial systems, depending on the type of crime committed and depending on where the crime occurs. If he commits a crime on deeded land he is subject to state jurisdiction. If he commits a crime on trust land it depends on the nature of the offense. A major crime, or felony committed on trust land, would subject him to federal jurisdiction under the Major Crimes Act. A misdemeanor committed on trust land would subject him to tribal jurisdiction. It is not uncommon for an Indian to flee from the town of Martin to the tribal housing area at Sunrise Housing if approached by a city police officer. Once he arrives at Sunrise Housing, he is on tribal land, where the state has no authority. Should he leave Sunrise Housing, however, he may be again approached by the city sheriff and processed through the state system in Martin.

Conversely, if a white person commits a crime on deeded land, he is subject to state jurisdiction regardless of who the victim is. If he commits a crime on trust land he may be subject to state or federal jurisdiction depending on the status of his victim. If his victim is Indian and the crime occurs on trust land, he would be subject to federal jurisdiction under the General Crimes Act. If he commits a crime on trust land against another white person, he is subject to state jurisdiction under a court-made law that extends state jurisdiction onto Indian reservations if both the perpetrator and the victim are white.

It is very unlikely that lawmakers foresaw the confusion they created by selling county land that was actually occupied by Indians on trust allotments. Trust land in the county could not be lawfully ceded to white settlers, unless allotted land was actually taken from the Indian occupant who held the land under the Allotment Act. Many Indians refused to leave Bennett County and have remained on their allotted land. Fortunately, they were not forcibly removed, which would have been another violation of the treaty. Since the acquisition of Bennett County and other parts of South Dakota Indian reservations was done without obtaining the consent of 3/4ths of all adult male Indians as required by Article 12 of the Fort Laramie Treaty, the taking of these lands was a violation of the treaty. Thus, the forcible taking of allotted land from Indian allottees would result in one treaty violation on top of another treaty violation.

Bennett County presents a unique problem to the Oglala Sioux Tribal government. It is "off reservation", except for the trust lands. The community of Allen, SD, a political district of the tribe, is located in Bennett County. Bennett County itself is home to tribal members who reside in the LaCreek District, which is a political district of the tribe. Thus, there are tribal council representatives from two districts in Bennett County, which is off the reservation, because Allen, SD is on trust lands, the representatives from Martin usually reside on trust lands, and there is little inquiry into the actual residence of a given tribal council member or officer. The tribe has acquiesced to the notion that the state is present within the original boundaries of the reservation. Additionally, the Oglala Sioux Tribe has recognized LaCreek District according to custom law. While federal law provides that Martin is no longer a part of the reservation, the tribe continues to recognize the tribal members who reside in Martin as reservation residents. And residents of Martin continue to behave as reservation residents; they vote in tribal elections, run for tribal office, and ignore the fact that federal law and federal case law have declared the Pine Ridge reservation to be "diminished" and stripped of the town of Martin, SD.

The Jake and Alice Herman Family Experience.

Many families suffered personal tragedies because of the government's policy of allotting land to Indians, selling off unallotted reservation lands to white homesteaders, and even taking Indian lands that were allotted and occupied by Indian families. An example of this governmental atrocity involved the appropriation of the badlands area on the Pine Ridge Reservation for bombing practice. In 1942, the Secretary of War, Henry Stimson, issued a directive to the War Department to acquire land needed for an aerial gunnery range. The War Department selected the badlands area in the northwestern part of the Pine Ridge Reservation. This area was chosen because of its location near the air base in Rapid City, its topography, and lack of railroads and major highways. The fact that the land was home to some 125 Indian families did nothing to stop the War Department from seizing the land for practicing bombing raids. Targets consisting of old car bodies were placed in circles on the ground for the U.S. Air Corps pilots to practice their bombing raids. One of the families who occupied a ranch in the badlands was the Jacob and Alice Herman (nee Janis) family. The families were given thirty days to move out of the area so that bombing could commence. They were able to negotiate a thirty-day extension, but all families had to leave or risk being exposed to aerial bombing raids. The time was late summer, when crops were ripe for picking and preserving. The produce had to be left to waste. Cattle and horses were herded up and relocated to other parts of the reservation. The Herman family packed up their belongings and moved to No Flesh Creek near Kyle, SD, where they lived in a tent until they were able to construct suitable shelter.

Shortly after this event, eighteen year-old Jacob "Sonny" Herman volunteered for the U.S. Army, and was inducted into the 82nd Airborne. He trained at Fort Benning, Georgia, and returned home on furlough before leaving for Europe. While spending time at home, Sonny informed his family that he would be parachuting behind German lines. At that time, a volunteer could opt out of parachuting during time of war, and his mother asked him to do so. Sonny told his mother that she had raised him "not to be a quitter" and that he intended to keep his commitment to the 82nd Airborne. His mother's fears for Sonny's safety, unfortunately, came true. Sonny was killed in action in 1944 at the age of nineteen years, during a reconnaissance mission in Operation Market Garden. He lies buried in a U.S. military cemetery in Holland.

Sonny is remembered for his love and devotion to his mother, father, brothers Rex and Paul, sisters Faith, Grace (deceased), and Hope. When the family relocated from the badlands to No Flesh, there was not enough room in the wagon for the cast iron stove that was used for cooking and heating. Sonny traveled by team and wagon back to the old badlands homesite, loaded up the stove by himself, and hauled it back to the new homesite. It was an eighty-mile round trip; he was only seventeen years old at the time, and the stove must have weighted over four hundred pounds, but he managed to retrieve his mother's most valuable household item. His mother grieved the loss of her son for the rest of her days. When she was informed that Sonny had been killed in Europe, she tearfully and sorrowfully remarked, "Our son gave his life defending the country that took our home."

The Kyle community soon learned of the Herman family loss. Mrs. Rough Feather, a survivor of the Wounded Knee Massacre, would travel near the Herman home each evening and would sing in Lakota the Akicita-Warrior Honoring song. In typical communal compassion, she would join the family as they wept and prayed for Sonny. In his family's eyes, Sonny is a true Lakota war hero. He loved his family and displayed all the attributes of Lakota spirituality, humility, kindness, and honesty. The United States government broke many treaties it made with the Lakota Nation, took his family's allotted land, shelled and bombed that land, and forced them to move from their home; but he loved his country and made the ultimate sacrifice. He is one of the many Lakota warriors who defended our native lands. (Source—Herman family members.)

Ironically, there are more Native Americans who volunteer for military service than any other ethnic group in the United States. Sonny's brother Rex served honorably in the United States Marine Corps, as did Paul who served in the U.S. Navy. Many other Herman family members served in all branches of the military. Native Americans dislike the U.S. government for its treatment of Indians, but they are very patriotic when it comes to defending the homelands. Protection of the homelands is a carryover from the days when warriors were honored and respected by the various Lakota bands, and the cultural belief that it is honorable to fight for one's country still exists.

CHAPTER SIX

Indian Reorganization Act of 1934

(Wheeler-Howard Act)

When the Great Depression occurred in 1929, the entire nation was in an economic tailspin. The stock market crashed, farms were unproductive because of the great drought, banks were foreclosing on worthless farms, and the United States needed to change its economic policies. In 1932, Franklin Delano Roosevelt was elected as President of the United States. He appointed John Collier as the Commissioner of Indian Affairs. Collier had been a social worker on one of the Pueblo reservations in New Mexico. Collier reported to Congress that the Indian allotment policy had been a total failure, that Indians had lost 90 million acres of land under the policy, and that the Indians needed an economic boost along with the rest of the nation. Senators Wheeler and Howard then sponsored the Indian Reorganization Act of 1934, and this spearheaded a sweeping change in the administration of Indian affairs.

Wheeler-Howard Act, June 18, 1934—The Indian Reorganization Act

Sec. 1 "BE IT ENACTED by the Senate and House of Representative of the United States of America in Congress assembled, That hereafter no land of any Indian reservation, created or set apart by treaty or agreement with the Indian, Act of Congress, Executive Order, purchase, or otherwise, shall be allotted in severalty to any Indian."

This portion of the IRA was too little, too late. The vast majority of Indians on the reservation had opposed allotment of reservation lands, but Congress paid no heed to them. By the time Congress stopped the practice of allotting land to individual Indians, most of the land had been lost. According to Janet McDonald, a historian for the U.S. Army Corps of Engineers, in 1934 two-thirds of the Indian population was either landless or didn't own enough to make a subsistence living. Janet McDonald is the author of a 1991 book, "Dispossession of the American Indian, 1887-1934".

Sec. 2 "The existing periods of trust placed upon any Indian lands and any restriction on alienation thereof are hereby extended and continued until otherwise directed by Congress."

The General Allotment Act provided that Indian land would be held in trust for a period of 25 years. The extension of the trust period to Indian lands in 1934 continues to this day.

Sec. 3 "The Secretary of the Interior, if he shall find it to be in the public interest, is hereby authorized to restore to tribal ownership the remaining surplus lands of any Indian reservation heretofore opened, or authorized to be opened, to sale, or any other form of disposal by Presidential proclamation, or by any of the public land laws of the United States: Provided however, That valid rights or claims of any persons to any lands so withdrawn existing on the date of the withdrawal shall not be affected by this Act . . . ."

"Surplus" lands in Section 3 refer to unalloted Indian land. There was no "surplus" because all eligible Indians did not receive allotments under the Allotment Act. Section 3 does close off the remaining Indian lands to white settlers wishing to claim reservation land. Thus, the Tribe became the owner of all unalloted Indian land on the reservation.

Sec. 4 "Except as herein provided, no sale, devise, gift, exchange or other transfer of restricted Indian lands or of shares in the assets of any Indian tribe or corporation organized hereunder, shall be made or approved: Provided, however, that such lands or interests may, with the approval of the Secretary of the Interior, be sold, devised, or otherwise transferred to the Indian tribe in which the lands or shares are located or from which the shares were derived or to a successor corporation, and in all instances such lands or interests shall descend or be devised, in accordance with the then existing laws of the State, or Federal laws where applicable, in which said lands are located or in which the subject matter of the corporation is located, to any member of such tribe or of such corporation or any heirs of such member: Provided further, that the Secretary of the Interior may authorize voluntary exchanges of lands of equal value and the voluntary exchange of shares of equal value whenever such exchange in his judgment is expedient and beneficial for or compatible with the proper consolidation of Indian lands and for the benefit of cooperative organizations."

Section 4 allows for the sale and transfer of Indian land to Indians or Indian tribes. It also provides that State probate laws shall apply in cases of descent and distribution. This provision brings in the substantive law of the state to determine the heirs of a decedent who dies without leaving a will. It is not a grant of state jurisdiction, but it requires the B.I.A. Administrative Law Judge to refer to state law in determining heirs for the descent and distribution of estate property. Congress has recently enacted probate laws for Indian lands, whereby the oldest child inherits the property of a decedent who dies without leaving a will. This is intended to address the problem of fractionated interests that have plagued the B. I. A., the tribes, and tribal members. For years, the descendants of allottees who die without leaving a will have inherited equal shares of the allotment, which has resulted in thousands of tribal members who own a share of the allotment, which in turn is a fraction of the original allotment. The Cobell lawsuit against the United States resulted in a 2012 settlement of $3.4 billion being awarded to some 500,000 tribal members who own fractionated interests in allotments, but have never received an accurate accounting of how their land was being managed by the B. I. A. over the years.

Sec. 5 "The Secretary of the Interior is hereby authorized in his discretion, to acquire through purchase, relinquishment, gift, exchange, or assignment, any interest in lands, water rights or surface rights to lands, within or without existing reservations, including trust or otherwise restricted allotments whether the allottee be living or deceased, for the purpose of providing lands for Indians.

For the acquisition of such lands, interests in lands, . . . there is herby authorized to be appropriated, out of any funds in the Treasury not otherwise appropriated, a sum not to exceed $2,000,000 in any one fiscal year: Provided that no part of such funds shall be used to acquire additional land outside the exterior boundaries of Navajo Indian Reservation for the Navajo Indians in Arizona and New Mexico, in the event that the proposed Navajo boundary extension measures now pending in congress and embodied the bills to define the exterior boundaries of the Navajo Indian Reservation, and for other purposes, and the bills to define the exterior boundaries of the Navajo Indian Reservation in New Mexico and for other purposes, or similar legislation, become law . . . . Title to any lands or rights acquired pursuant to this Act shall be taken in the name of the United States in trust for the Indian tribe or individual Indian for which the land is acquired, and such lands or rights shall be exempt from State and local taxation."

Section 5 authorizes the Secretary to provide land for Indian tribes except for the Navajo. The reason for the Navajo exception is that the Navajo Indian Reservation increased in size while the other Indian reservations decreased in size over the years. Around 1884, the Navajos were held captive at Fort Sumner located in eastern New Mexico. They had been forced to surrender to Kit Carson at Canyon DeChelley near Chinle, Arizona. After being in captivity for some four years, the Navajos negotiated their treaty of 1868 with the United States. They were released to return to their homelands, which were described in the treaty. The boundary lines were described on paper, but were not visible on the surface of the land. As a result, the Navajos settled outside their defined boundaries in areas surrounding the treaty reservation. The Secretary of the Interior elected to add those areas to the reservation by Executive Order, instead of forcing the tribal members out of the areas in which they had trespassed. Consequently, the Navajo Reservation had grown to approximately four times its original size. When the IRA was passed in 1934 to authorize additional lands for existing Indian reservations, the Navajo reservation was exempted because they did not experience the problem that other tribes experienced in losing their land to white settlers.

Section 5 (465) is Congressional approval for the Secretary through the President to add lands to existing reservations, including the Lakota reservations. That authority was challenged in 1995, when the Attorney General for State of South Dakota challenged the Secretary's authority to allow the Lower Brule Sioux Tribe to purchase 91 acres of off-reservation land at Oacoma, SD, and add it to their reservation. The U. S. District Court and the Eighth Circuit Court of Appeals agreed that Section 465 was unconstitutional, because it granted unrestricted power to the Secretary of the Interior to acquire land to be placed in trust for Indian tribes. The federal lawyers appealed to the Supreme Court. Section 465 was upheld by the Supreme Court when it vacated the judgment order of the Eight Circuit Court, and remanded the matter back to the Secretary with instructions to give notice and an opportunity for a hearing to the State before purchasing lands to be placed into trust for an Indian tribe. Ironically, no one challenged the Government's authority to take Indian land, remove it from the reservation and change its legal status from trust to deeded land. When the situation is reversed, the Indian tribe has to defend what rights it did receive through the IRA because the State is in danger of losing property tax revenue from land once it is placed back into trust. The IRA provision is presently intact; but it is more cumbersome for a tribal member to purchase deeded reservation land and put it in trust. There is now a process whereby the local States Attorney is notified if a tribal member wishes to put deeded land in trust: a hearing is held and due process procedures are followed so that deeded reservation land can be put back into trust status. Section 5 is filled with good intentions, but very little land has actually been returned to the tribes.

Much has been written about treaty violations, government theft of Indian land, government mishandling of Indian property, and government violation of its trust responsibility. So much of it has been written about and discussed that it seems to be accepted as normal behavior on the part of the United States. People tend to shake their heads and agree that the government was or is in the wrong for mistreating the Indians, massacring the Indians, cheating the Indians, stealing from the Indians, and so on. After all is said and done, it is time for remedial action to address the most egregious of the government's crimes against Indians.

Section 465 of the IRA can be seen as authority for the President to return the federal lands in the Black Hills to the treaty tribes. Since the Supreme Court affirmed the decision of the Court of Claims and ruled that the land was taken in violation of the treaty, the President has good authority to act in the interest of justice and to return at least the federal lands in the Black Hills to the treaty nations involved in the Fort Laramie Treaty of 1868. The Executive Branch is the only remaining branch of government that can help. In 1985, the Black Hills Steering Committee submitted a bill sponsored by Senator Bill Bradley of New Jersey. The Bradley Bill required a senatorial sponsor and no South Dakota senator would touch it. Senators Tom Daschle and Larry Pressler refused to support the legislation that proposed to return the federal lands in the Black Hills to the Sioux, but to allow the federal government to continue managing the land for the treaty tribes. There is a policy referred to as "senatorial courtesy" whereby the senators of the affected state must first support the legislation before it will be accepted by the appropriate committee. The South Dakota senators apparently believed that their constituents would be greatly offended if they supported such a measure, and they would not touch it. Senator Bill Bradley, the former NBA star who was a senator from New Jersey at the time, agreed to sponsor the bill. Of course, the bill never left committee, and it died without ever reaching Congress. There would be no legislative remedy. The federal courts were without authority to return property, as their jurisdiction limited their remedies to monetary judgment awards only. The Executive Branch is the only conceivable branch of government that can do the right thing. The Lakota people have long believed that when a person steals your property, you can go to court with a complaint, and that if the court agrees with you and finds that the thief illegally stole your property, then you should be entitled to recover the property provided that the thief still has the property in his possession. That is the general rule of law that is supposed to apply in the "land of the free", where liberty and justice prevail. The United States is the first to preach to other countries about its own humanity, its generosity, its belief in democracy and human rights. But unless the United States is willing to return a portion of the Black Hills which it stole from the Indians, its preaching is nothing but rhetoric, and its actions amount to nothing but hypocrisy.

Mount Rushmore monument is situated in the center of the Black Hills. The granite faces of Washington, Lincoln, Roosevelt and Jefferson are referred to as the "Shrine of Democracy". These four U.S Presidents supposedly represent American ideals, and as such, it is ironic that this monument sits on stolen land. It would, in fact, be more appropriately referred to as the "Shrine of Hypocrisy".

Sec. 6 "The Secretary of the Interior is directed to make rules and regulations for the operation and management of Indian forestry units on the principle of sustained-yield management, to restrict the number of livestock grazed on Indian range units to the estimated carrying capacity of such ranges, and to promulgate such other rules and regulations as may be necessary to protect the range from deterioration, to prevent soil erosion, to assure full utilization of the range, and like purposes."

If federal lands are ever returned to the treaty tribes, the Secretary would be charged with the responsibility of managing the forest and grazing lands within the areas. The BIA agencies staff and operate a Department of Land Management with the responsibility of assuring that Indian trust land is properly maintained. Grazing regulations prohibit those who lease and use Indian range units from overgrazing or otherwise misusing the land, and there have been cases where cattle ranchers have had to pay huge fines for overgrazing the land.

Sec. 7 "The Secretary of the Interior is hereby authorized to proclaim new Indian reservations on lands acquired pursuant to any authority conferred by this Act, or to add such lands to existing reservations: Provided, that lands added to existing reservations shall be designated for the exclusive use of Indians entitled by enrollment or by tribal membership to residence at such reservations shall be designated for the exclusive use of Indians entitled by enrollment or by tribal membership o residence at such reservations."

Section 7 reflects a drastic reversal of the previous allotment policy. The establishment of new Indian reservations and enlargement of existing Indian reservations is well-intentioned, and would be very beneficial to the tribes if these policies were actually carried out. There is at least one, and probably more, new Indian reservation that was established since 1934. An Apache Indian reservation located in the Tonto National Forest in Arizona was established in the 1960's under Section 7 of the IRA.

Sec. 8 "Nothing contained in this Act shall be construed to relate to Indian holdings of allotments or homesteads upon the public domain outside of the geographic boundaries of any Indian reservation now existing or established hereafter."

Section 8 can be interpreted to mean that an individual Indian allotment or ownership of land in the state that is outside the boundaries of the reservation may not be considered to be a part of the reservation. An exception to this provision is the trust land in Bennett County that is Indian-owned. Under the Act of May 27, 1910, and the decision in Cook v. Parkinson, trust land in Bennett County is considered a part of the reservation. The best example is the community of Allen, SD. It is a tribal community consisting of tribal district office, Oglala Sioux Lakota Housing area, Oglala Lakota College Center, American Horse School; and its tribal member residents participate in tribal political activities and receive tribal governmental services. For all intents and purposes, Allen is within the boundaries of the Pine Ridge Indian Reservation according to tribal law, but is outside the "diminished" reservation according to federal law. In this case, the tribal law trumps federal law because both governments recognize and acknowledge Allen, SD and other trust land in Bennett County as tribal land.

Sec. 9 "There is hereby authorized to be appropriated, out of any funds in the Treasury not otherwise appropriated, such sums as may be necessary, but not to exceed $250,000 in any fiscal year, to be expended at the order of the Secretary of the Interior, in defraying the expenses of organizing Indian chartered corporations or other organizations created under this Act."

Chartered organizations of the Oglala Sioux Tribe include Oglala Sioux Lakota Housing, Inc., Oglala Lakota College, OST Department of Public Safety, and others including most reservation-based schools. The Tribe grants charters to these organizations under its constitutional power to charter subordinate organizations.

Sec. 10 "There is hereby authorized to be appropriated, out of funds in the Treasury not otherwise appropriated, the sum of $10,000 to be established as a revolving fund from which the Secretary of the Interior, under such rules and regulations as he may prescribe, may make loans to Indian chartered corporations for the purpose of promoting the economic development of such tribes and of their members, and may defray the expenses of administering such loans. Repayment of amounts loaned under this authorization shall be credited to the revolving fund and shall be available for the purposes for which the fund is established. A report shall be made annually to Congress of transactions under this authorization.

There is little information available from the Credit Office regarding loans to tribally chartered organizations. Ten thousand dollars would contribute very little to the economic development of tribes and their members, although small loans were made to individuals in the early days for farm and ranching operations.

Sec. 11 "There is hereby authorized to be appropriated, out of any funds in the United States Treasury not otherwise appropriated, a sum not to exceed $250,000 annually, together with any unexpended balances of previous appropriations made pursuant to this section, for loans to Indians for the payment of tuition and other expenses in recognized vocational and trade schools: Provided, that not more than

$50,000 of such sum shall be available for loans to Indian students in high schools and colleges. Such loans shall be reimbursable under rules established by the Commissioner of Indian Affairs.

Article 7 of the Fort Laramie Treaty promised the Indians an "English education" to insure the civilization of the Indians entering into the treaty. The treaty referred to the primary educational years of children between the ages of 6 and 16. Provision was made for education beyond the elementary and high school years under Section 11 of the IRA, and appears to be the forerunner to the student loan program. Eventually, it became easier for Indian students to afford college and vocational training with funding sources provided from the U.S. Department of Education. Most Indian college students now utilize the Pell grant, and there are scholarships and other grants available to those to aspire to higher learning objectives. Thousands of Indian veterans of the armed services attended college under the GI Bill, and moved on to successful careers.

Sec. 12 "The Secretary of the Interior is directed to establish standards of health, age, character, experience, knowledge, and ability for Indians who maybe appointed, without regard to civil-service laws, to the various positions maintained, now or hereafter, by the Indian office, in the administration's functions or services affecting any Indian tribe. Such qualified Indians shall hereafter have the preference to appointment to vacancies in such positions."

In a landmark case, *Morton v. Mancari,* the Supreme Court upheld the constitutionality of the Section 12 Indian Preference statutes. The Indian preference policy was applied strictly to initial appointment only, until 1972 when the Secretary decided to extend Indian preference to promotions of Indian employees already employed in the Bureau of Indian Affairs. A group of non-Indian BIA employees challenged Indian preference as being repealed by the 1972 Equal Employment Opportunity Act, and alleged that Indian preference deprived them of due process of law in violation of the Fifth Amendment to the Constitution of the United States.

The lower court agreed with the plaintiffs, but the Supreme Court reversed its order and declared that Indian preference is a valid exercise of Congress' power defined in Article 1 of the Constitution. Article 1 empowers Congress "to regulate commerce . . . with Indian Tribes." The Court quoted Senate sponsor Hubert Humphrey as saying "This exemption is consistent with the Federal Government's policy of encouraging Indian employment and with the special legal position of Indians." (110 Con. Rec. 2723 (1964)

The Court also referred to other Indian preference laws that were adopted around the same time that the Secretary extended Indian preference to promotions within the Bureau.

The Education Amendments of 1972 authorized funding for teacher training programs to Indians who aspire to teach Indian children. In fact, many of the present day tribal community colleges began as teacher training programs offered in satellite campuses from surrounding colleges and universities that were brought to the Indian reservations. OLC was first named the Lakota Higher Education Learning Center, then Oglala Community College, and finally, Oglala Lakota College. Sicangu University on the Rosebud Indian Reservation had a similar experience, as did Si Tonka University at Cheyenne River, and Sitting Bull College on the Standing Rock reservation.

It is not difficult for Lakota people to understand its unique legal status under federal law. After all, who are parties to the treaties with the United States? Whose land did the United States purchase and otherwise acquire under treaties and laws that apply only to Indians? The federal Major Crimes Act applies only to Indians who commit crimes on the reservation and no one else. The fact that the government prefers to employ qualified Indians to serve other Indians is recognition that Indians know Indians better than do others. The more recent policy of Indian self-determination was enunciated by President Richard Nixon, and has been the existing federal Indian policy since 1970 when he first announced the policy to Congress.

The federal constitution recognizes Indians as a distinct class of citizens, which Congress alone can manage. The Courts have defined this relationship in various ways. It has been referred to as a "trust" relationship, or one that resembles that of a ward to his guardian. Inasmuch as the Indian is mentioned specifically in the constitution, Indian tribes are said to have a "unique legal status", meaning that laws can be made that apply only to Indians and not necessarily everyone else. It is therefore constitutional and lawful for Congress to enact laws that are sometimes beneficial to Indians, which over the years have been very rare at best.

Sec. 13 "The provisions of this Act shall not apply to any of the Territories, colonies of insular possessions of the United States, except that Sections 9, 10, 11, 12, and 16 shall apply to the Territory of Alaska; Provided, that Sections 2, 4, 7, 16, 17, and 18 of this Act shall not apply to the following named Indian tribes, together with members of other tribes affiliated with such named located in the State of Oklahoma, as follows: Cheyenne, Arapaho, Apache, Comanche, Kiowa, Caddo, Delaware, Wichita, Osage, Kaw, Otoe, Tonkawa, Pawnee, Ponca, Shawnee, Ottawa, Quapaw, Chickasaw, Choctaw, Creek and Seminole. Section 4 of this Act shall not apply to the Indians of the Klamath Reservation in Oregon."

All provisions of the IRA apply to the Lakota.

Sec. 14 "The Secretary of the Interior is hereby directed to continue the allowance of articles enumerated in Section 17 of the Act of March 2, 1889 (25 Stat. L. 891), or their commuted cash value under the Act of June 10, 1886 (29 Stat L. 334), to all Sioux Indians who would be eligible, but for the provisions of this Act, to receive allotments of lands in severalty under section 19 of the Act of May 29, 1908, (25 Stat. L. 451), or under any prior Act, and who have the prescribed status of the head of a family or single person over the age of eighteen years, and his approval shall be final and conclusive, claims therefore to be paid as formerly from the permanent appropriation made by said section 17 and carried on the books of the Treasury for this purpose. No person shall receive in his own right more than one allowance of the benefits, and application must be made and approved during the lifetime of the allottee or the right shall lapse. Such benefits shall continue to be paid upon such reservation until such time as the lands available therein for allotment at the time of the passage of this act would have been exhausted by the award to each person receiving such benefits of an allotment of eighty acres of such land."

Application of Section 14 is obsolete. Anyone entitled to an allotment prior to 1934 who did not receive an allotment would be entitled to compensation under the Act of March 2, 1889. The Act of March 2, 1889 is the statute that divided what was left of the Great Sioux Reservation into the five West River Lakota Tribes. Most of the remaining Indian land was taken so that the Territory of South Dakota would be able to achieve statehood and lay claim to most of the lands west of the Missouri River and beyond the Black Hills. Consequently, this section of the IRA is also obsolete.

Sec. 15 "Nothing in this Act shall be construed to impair or prejudice any claim or suit of any Indian tribe against the United States. It is hereby declared to be the intent of Congress that no expenditures for the benefit of Indians made out of appropriations authorized by this Act shall be considered as offsets in any suit brought to recover upon any claim of such Indians against the United States."

Sioux Nation of Indians v United States (the Black Hills case) was pending at the time this statute was enacted. Even though the statutes provides that lawsuits against the United States would not be impaired, government lawyers argued that appropriations made to the Sioux Nation after the Black Hills were taken should be considered offsets, which means that the amount of expenditures made by the United States should reduce the amount of any judgment awards made to the Sioux for the unlawful taking of the Black Hills.

Congress passed the Sioux Jurisdictional Act on June 3, 1920. Congress passed other jurisdictional acts that year for other tribes. The Lakota tribes were not completely satisfied with the statute, but it did open the courthouse door for them to file a lawsuit for the taking of the Black Hills.

It was necessary for the Sioux to wait until 1920, when Congress responded to demands that the federal courts be empowered to hear claims of treaty violations by Indian tribes. The problem with the jurisdictional acts is that the only remedy the federal courts were authorized to make was monetary compensation, and not a return of property.

Another obstacle to filing of the claim was the *Lone Wolf v. Hitchcock* case. In 1903, Lone Wolf filed a claim in U. S. District Court claiming that the Secretary of the Interior sold land that was described in the Medicine Lodge Treaty of 1867. The Medicine Lodge Treaty was similar to the Fort Laramie Treaty of 1868. Article 12 of both treaties provided that "No treaty for the cession of any portion or part of the reservation herein described which may be held in common, shall be of any validity or force as against the said Indians unless executed and signed by at least three-fourths of all adult male Indians occupying or interested in the same . . ."

Lone Wolf complained that the Secretary had sold off a portion of the reservation belonging to the Kiowa, Comanche, and Apache tribes of Oklahoma without obtaining the consent of three-fourths of all adult male Indians of the tribes. Lone Wolf's complaint was that the Secretary had violated Article 12 of the Medicine Lodge Treaty. The court dismissed the case and the Supreme Court affirmed the decision. The dismissal of the case by the federal courts set a legal precedent that prevented the Sioux from filing a claim against the United States for the same violation. It wasn't until 1920 that Congress waived its sovereign immunity from suit and allowed Indian tribes to file claims for treaty violations.

In the Lone Wolf case, the Supreme Court ruled that Congress had plenary (supreme) power to regulate commerce with Indian tribes as stated in the constitution, and that selling of Indian land was "management" not to be questioned by the Court. The Court went on to say that it must presume that Congress acted in perfect good faith when it takes Indian land in violation of a treaty and that the actions of Congress are deemed to be "political" in nature. The Court simply ruled that Congressional taking of Indian land in violation is political in nature, and does not present a legal question for the courts to decide. In other words, Congress can do what it wants and the Courts will not question the motives of Congress, which it presumes to act in good faith. Because Congress possessed full power to manage Indian affairs, the Court would not question the legislation passed by Congress. The Court concluded that Indian tribes must appeal to Congress, and not the courts, if they want redress for treaty violations.

The Lakota people knew that Congress violated Article 12 of the treaty; but in a land where Congress rules supreme, there was no relief in sight. It is ironic that the colonists and framers of the Constitution were subjected to the same kinds of treatment that the Indians experienced, but instead of dispensing justice and fairness according to constitutional principles, it chose to ignore the rights of Indian tribes. Within the entire government, from the President to Congress to the Courts, the American ideal of "liberty and justice for all" was lost when it came to dealing with the first Americans. Thus, it is clear that several forces motivated the United States to treat Native Americans the way it did—greed, racism, and imperialism.

Sec. 16 "Any Indian tribe, or tribes, residing on the same reservation, shall have the right to organize for its common welfare, and may adopt an appropriate constitution and bylaws, which shall become effective when ratified by a majority vote of the adult members of the tribe, or of the adult Indians residing on such reservation, as the case may be, at a special election authorized by the Secretary of the Interior under such rules and regulations as he may prescribe. Such constitution and bylaws when ratified as aforesaid and approved by the Secretary of the Interior shall be revocable by an election open to the same voters and conducted in the same manner as hereinabove provided. Amendments to the constitution and bylaws may be ratified and approved by the Secretary in the same manner as the original constitution and bylaws.

In addition to all powers vested in any Indian tribe or tribal council by existing law, the constitution adopted by said tribe shall also vest in such tribe or its tribal council the following rights and powers: To employ legal counsel, the choice of counsel and fixing of fees to the subject to the approval of the Secretary of the Interior; to prevent the sale, disposition, lease, or encumbrance of tribal lands, interests in lands or other tribal assets without the consent of the tribe; and to negotiate with the Federal, State and local Governments. The Secretary of the Interior shall advise such tribe or its tribal council of all appropriation estimates or Federal projects for the benefit of the tribe prior to the submission of such estimates to the Bureau of the Budget and the Congress."

Section 16 is often cited in ordinances and resolutions enacted by the tribal council. The Oglala Sioux Tribe adopted its constitution and by-laws in a referendum vote on December 14, 1935. A total of 1,348 tribal members voted in favor of the constitution, and a total of 1,041 voted against adopting the constitution. The ratification of the constitution by a majority of the voter was approved and the constitution has been in effect since its final approval. On January 7, 1936, John Collier, Commissioner of Indian Affairs, recommended approval and the first Constitution and By-Laws of the Oglala Sioux Tribe under the IRA was approved on January 15, 1936. The constitution has undergone several amendments since its birth. It was amended in the years 1969, 1985, 1997, and in 2008.

Sec. 17 "The Secretary of the Interior may, upon petition by at least one-third of the adult Indians, issue a charter of incorporation to such tribe: Provided, that such charter shall not become operative until ratified at a special election by a majority vote of the adult Indians living on the reservation. Such charter may convey to the incorporated tribe the power to purchase, take by gift, or bequest, or otherwise, own, hold, manage, operate, and dispose of property of every description, real and personal, including the power to purchase restricted Indian lands and to issue in exchange therefore interests in corporate property, and such further powers as may be incidental to the conduct of corporate business, not inconsistent with law, but no authority shall be granted to sell, mortgage, or lease for a period exceeding ten years any of the land included in the limits of the reservation. Any charter so issued shall not be revoked or surrendered except by Act of Congress."

Section 17 authorizes a tribe to incorporate under the IRA but has not been implemented due to the requirement that at least one third of all adult Indians petition the Secretary for a charter. Most corporations other than tribal chartered organizations are organized under nonprofit provisions of 501-(3)c.

Sec. 18 "This Act shall not apply to any reservation wherein a majority of the adult Indians, voting at a special election duly called by the Secretary of the Interior, shall vote against its application. It shall be the duty of the Secretary of the Interior, within one year after the passage and approval of this Act, to call such an election, which election shall be held by secret ballot upon thirty days' notice."

The Oglala Sioux Tribe voted to accept the Wheeler-Howard Bill as early as 1933,

Sec. 19 "The term "Indian" as used in this Act shall include all persons of Indian descent who are members of any recognized Indian tribe now under Federal jurisdiction, and all persons who are descendants of such members who were, on June 1, 1934, residing within the present boundaries of any reservation, and shall further include all other persons of one-half or more Indian blood. For the purposes of this Act, Eskimos and other aboriginal peoples of Alaska shall be considered Indians. The term "tribe" whenever used in this Act shall be construed to refer to any Indian tribe, organized band, pueblo, or the Indians residing on one reservation. The words "adult Indians" wherever used in this Act shall be construed to refer to Indians who have attained the age of twenty-one years."

Section 19 defines an "Indian" for federal purposes. The statute does not state who shall be considered an Indian, but leaves that decision with the tribe. If an Indian tribe recognizes a person to be one of its members, then that recognition satisfies the federal government's authority to treat that person as an "Indian" who would then be eligible for services provided to Indians by the federal government. It is also important for the federal government to know whether a person is a recognized "Indian" for purposes of federal jurisdiction.

CHAPTER SEVEN

CONSTITUTION AND BY-LAWS
OF THE OGLALA SIOUX TRIBE

The experiences of the Indian tribes differ greatly from those of the United States in framing a constitution to meet their needs. After the initial articles of the U.S. Constitution were drafted, the Bill of Rights was added to the U.S. Constitution specifically to address problems the settlers had experienced in European nations. The Bill of Rights was designed to prevent government intrusion into the personal lives of U. S. citizens. Oppressive rulers had never governed the Lakota people. Decisions for the band were made by consensus of the people, who were free to participate in the group activities or to join another band of the Lakota nation. All practiced the same spiritual ceremonies, all participated in community activities and people were allowed to express their opinions without fear of retribution from those who disagreed with them. Private property was limited to horses, blankets, tools, and weapons. Food was shared by all, and there were no classes of haves and have-nots. Land was owned communally and was not regarded as real estate, but was instead preserved as hunting grounds. The buffalo belonged to Mother Earth, and she provided all the needs of the Lakota people. There was no need for a formal, written constitution, and none existed. The Lakota experienced a true democracy through their inherent sovereign authority to exist as a nation. The traditional Lakota government, as it existed, was truly of the people, by the people, and for the people. There was no need to improve on the traditional social and economic structure of the Lakota.

Tribal constitutions did not originate on Indian reservations, nor did the Indians decide that they should have a constitution to protect them from their governments. Hence, a formal governmental structure/hierarchy as such did not exist.

The Office of Indian Affairs drafted the tribal constitutions that were adopted in the 1930's. They are modeled loosely after the federal and state constitutions, but with major differences. The tribal constitutions did not contain a "Bill of Rights", nor did they contain a specific article establishing separation of powers between the legislative, executive, and judicial branches of government. The standard preamble, however, provides that the tribe ". . . in order to establish a more perfect organization, promote the general welfare, conserve and develop our lands and resources, secure to ourselves and our posterity the power to exercise certain rights of home rule not inconsistent with Federal laws and our treaties and in recognition of God Almighty and His Divine Providence do ordain and establish this constitution for the Oglala Sioux Tribe." The reference to Federal laws implies intent to govern through powers that are separate from each branch—Legislative, Executive, and Judicial.

The following is a summary of the current Constitution and By-laws of the Oglala Sioux Tribe. Other Lakota Tribes—Cheyenne River, Rosebud, Lower Brule, and Standing Rock adopted similar constitutions that have been amended from time to time over the years.

The tribal constitution presented to each tribe was a generic model that contained the same provisions, except for the name of the tribe and the political districts. Over the years, each tribe has amended its constitution as its needs changed.

PREAMBLE

We, the Oglala Sioux Tribe of the Pine Ridge Indian Reservation, in order to establish a more perfect organization, promote the general welfare, conserve and develop our lands and resources, secure to ourselves and our posterity the power to exercise certain rights of home rule not inconsistent with Federal laws and our treaties, and in recognition of God Almighty and His Divine Providence, do ordain and establish this constitution for the Oglala Sioux Tribe.

Article 1—TERRITORY. "The jurisdiction the Oglala Sioux Tribe of Indians shall extend to the territory within the original confines of the Pine Ridge Indian Reservation boundaries, as defined by the Act of March 2, 1889 (25 Stat L. 1888), and to such other lands as may be hereafter added thereto under any law of the United States except as may be other-wise provided by law for unrestricted lands."

Commentary: the original boundaries have been affected by the Act of May 27, 1910, which removed Bennett County from the Pine Ridge Reservation thus "diminishing" the size of the reservation by taking Bennett County out of the reservation and reducing the boundaries which had been established by Act of March 2, 1889.

Article I now reads: **"The jurisdiction of the Oglala Sioux Tribe of Indians shall extend to the territory within the original confines of the Pine Ridge Indian Reservation boundaries, as defined hereafter added thereto under any law of the**

United States except as may be otherwise provided by law for unrestricted lands to regulate the inheritance of property, real and personal, other than allotted lands, within the territory of the Pine Ridge Indian Reservation."

Article 2—MEMBERSHIP

Section 1. Membership in the Oglala Sioux Tribe shall be automatic when:

(a) The person's name appears on the official roll of the Oglala Sioux Tribe of the Pine Ridge Reservation as of April 1, 1935 or if the person's name appears on any correction made within five years after the adoption of the Constitution in January 1936.

(b) A child is born to any member of the Oglala Sioux Tribe.

Section 2. The Tribal Council shall have the authority to adopt laws covering future membership."

Commentary: The foregoing amendment was in response to problems that arose when members of the tribe resided off the reservation. Under the old provision, they could not be enrolled because they were not born on the reservation; hence, there were many Lakota families with children, some of whom were enrolled and others who were not.

Article 3—GOVERNING BODY

Section 1. The governing body of the tribe under this constitution shall be a council which shall be composed of councilmen chosen by secret ballot by qualified voters of the tribe, which council shall hereafter be known as "The Oglala Sioux Tribal Council."

Section 2. Each district of the reservation as follows, shall be entitled to representation on the tribal council according to population as hereinafter provided:

Oglala District: The tribal council shall prescribe boundaries by ordinance with local participation, through district hearings.

Wakpamni District: The tribal council shall describe boundaries by ordinance with local participation, through district hearings.

Wounded Knee District: The tribal council shall describe boundaries by ordinance with local participation, through district hearings.

Porcupine district: The tribal council shall describe boundaries by ordinance with local participation, through district hearings.

Medicine Root District. The tribal council shall describe boundaries by ordinance with local participation through district hearings.

Eagle Nest District: The tribal council shall describe boundaries by ordinance with local participation, through district hearings.

Pass Creek District: The tribal council shall describe boundaries by ordinance with local participation through district hearings.

LaCreek District: The tribal council shall describe boundaries by ordinance with local participation, through district hearings.

Pine Ridge District: The tribal council shall describe boundaries by ordinance with local participation through district hearings."

Commentary: There are a total of nine political districts on the Pine Ridge Reservation. Other tribes have varying numbers of political districts, but all are organized as such. Each political district is entitled to representation depending on the population of each district. Pine Ridge has the largest population on the reservation and presently has three council representatives.

District boundary lines are not visible, except on a map. Each district is aware of its boundaries, and district members know in which district they are residing. There have been very few changes since the original boundaries were established and the issue comes up at times, but is soon forgotten once the election is over. Students should refer to their tribal constitutions for a better understanding of their tribal political districts and membership requirements.

Section 3. "The tribal council shall have authority to make changes in the foregoing list according to future community needs, subject to the approval of the Secretary of the Interior."

Section 4. "Each recognized district shall elect representatives to the tribal council in the proportion of one representative for each 1,000 members or a remainder of more than 500. Recognized communities with less than 500 members shall be consolidated by the tribal council with an adjacent recognized community."

Commentary: The tribe has been unable to accommodate all districts with the requisite number of representatives per district. All districts have two representatives on the tribal council while Pine Ridge, the largest district, has three.

Section 5. "Prior to the first election of the tribal council, the membership of each district shall be determined by the Superintendent and a committee consisting of one delegate from each district herein designated. Thereafter the membership of the various districts shall be determined by the districts subject to review by the tribal council."

Section 6. "The officers of the tribal council shall be a president and a vice president, elected by the members of the Oglala Sioux Tribe, at large, and a secretary, a treasurer, and such other officers as may be deemed necessary, elected by the tribal council from within or outside of its own number. Officers elected from outside the membership of the council shall have no vote in the council, except that the president shall vote in case of a tie."

Section 7. "The first election of the tribal council hereunder shall be called and supervised by the Secretary of the Interior, or such persons as he may appoint."

Commentary: Section 7 has long been obsolete. With the change in federal Indian policy from early paternalism to self-determination, there has been virtually no involvement by the federal officers in tribal decision-making.

Section 8. "Members of the tribal council shall be elected for a term of two years."

Commentary: Some tribes have changed the terms of office to more than two years. The Oglalas have strictly followed section 8 since its inception.

Section 9. "Elections to tribal council, after the first election shall be called by the tribal council at least sixty days prior to the expiration of office of its members."

Section 10. "The Oglala Sioux Tribal Council shall be the sole judge of the constitutional qualifications of its own members."

ARTICLE IV—POWERS OF THE COUNCIL

Section 1. "Enumerated powers—The Oglala Sioux Tribal Council shall exercise the following powers, subject to any limitations imposed by the statutes or the

Constitution of the United States and subject further to all express restrictions upon such powers contained in this constitution and the attached by-laws."

(a) To negotiate with the Federal, State, and local governments, on behalf of the tribe, and to advise and consult with the representatives of the Interior Department on all activities of the Department that may affect the Pine Ridge Indian Reservation.

(b) To employ legal counsel for the protection and advancement of the rights of the Oglala Sioux Tribe and its members, the choice of counsel and fixing of fees subject to the approval of the Secretary of the Interior.

(c) To approve or veto any sale, disposition, lease or encumbrance of the tribal lands, interest in lands, or other tribal assets which may be authorized or executed by the Secretary of the Interior, the Commissioner of Indian Affairs, or any other authorized official or agency of government provided that no tribal lands shall eve be leased for a period exceeding five years, sold, or encumbered except for governmental purposes.

(d) To advise the Secretary of the Interior with regard to all appropriation estimates or Federal projects for the benefit of the Pine Ridge Indian Reservation prior to the submission of such estimates to the Bureau of the Budget and Congress.

(e) To make assignments of tribal land to members of the Oglala Sioux Tribe in conformity with Article X of this constitution

(f) To manage all economic affairs and enterprises of the Oglala Sioux Tribe in accordance with the terms of a charter that may be issued to the Tribe by the Secretary of the Interior.

(g) To appropriate for public purposes of the tribe any available tribal council funds.

(h) To levy taxes or license fees upon persons on the Pine Ridge Indian reservation and to require the performance of community labor in lieu thereof.

(i) To exclude from the restricted lands of the Pine Ridge Indian Reservation persons not legally entitled to reside therein under duly enacted ordinances. Amendment M, 2008: To remove trespassers, and exclude and banish persons from within the boundaries of the Pine Ridge Indian Reservation as defined in Article 1.

(j) To enact resolutions or ordinances not inconsistent with Article II of this constitution concerning membership in the Oglala Sioux Tribe.

(k) To promulgate and enforce ordinances governing the conduct of persons on the Pine Ridge Indian Reservation, and providing for the maintenance of law and order and the administration of justice by establishing a reservation court and defining its duties and powers.

(l) To purchase, under condemnation proceedings in courts of competent jurisdiction, land or other property needed for public purposes.

(m)To protect and preserve the property, wild-life, and natural resources, gases, oils, and other minerals, of the tribe, and to regulate the conduct of trade and the use and disposition of property upon the reservation.

(o) To cultivate native arts, crafts, and culture, to administer charity and to protect the health and general welfare of the tribe. Amendment Z, 2008—"To regulate, preserve, and strengthen native arts, crafts, culture, and the Lakota language."

(p) To charter subordinate organizations for economic purposes and to regulate the activities of associations thus chartered by the tribal council, or any other associates of members of the tribe, which are indebted to the tribe.

(q) To regulate the inheritance of property real and personal, other than allotted lands, within the territory of the Pine Ridge Indian Reservation.

(r) To regulate the domestic relations of members of the tribe.

(s) To provide for the appointment of guardians for minors and mental incompetents by ordinance or resolution.

(t) To adopt resolutions regulating the procedure of the council itself and of other tribal agencies and tribal officials of the reservation.

(u) To delegate to subordinate boards or officers or to cooperative associations which are open to all members of the tribe any of the foregoing powers, reserving the right to review any action taken by virtue of such delegated power.

(v) To adopt ordinances regulating the procedure of the council itself and of other elected officials of the reservation through a comprehensive code of ethics and removal procedures.

(w)To adopt an ordinance incorporating a bill of rights provision for all tribal members."

Section 2. "Future Powers—The council of the Oglala Sioux Tribe may exercise such further powers as may in the future be delegated to the council by members of the tribe or by the Secretary of the Interior, or any other duly authorized official or agency of the Federal Government.

Section 3. Reserved Powers—Any rights and powers heretofore vested in the Oglala Sioux Tribe, but not expressly referred to in this constitution, shall not be abridged by this article, but may be exercised by the people of the Oglala Sioux Tribe through the adoption of appropriate by-laws and constitutional amendments.

Commentary: Reserved powers belong exclusively to the people who may adopt amendments to the Constitution; the Reserved Powers clause does not increase the powers of the tribal council without a supporting amendment to the constitution that is approved by a majority of those tribal members expressed in a referendum vote.

ARTICLE V—JUDICAL POWERS

Section 1. "Creation. The Judicial power of the Oglala Sioux Tribe shall be vested in one Supreme Court and in other inferior tribal courts established by the Tribal Council. The Supreme Court and other inferior tribal courts shall be independent from the Tribal Council and the Executive Committee, and no elected official exercising powers of the Tribal Council or the Executive Committee shall exercise powers vested in the Supreme Court or other inferior tribal courts.

Section 2. "Jurisdiction. The judicial power shall extend to all cases, in law and equity, arising under the Oglala Sioux Tribe Constitution, the laws of the Oglala Sioux Tribe, or to all persons and property within the jurisdiction of the Oglala Sioux tribe.

Section 3. "Powers of the Supreme Court. The Supreme Court shall exercise the following powers:

> **(a) The Supreme Court shall have appellate jurisdiction over any case on appeal from inferior tribal courts.**
> **(b) The Supreme Court shall have the power to declare laws of the Oglala Sioux Tribe void if such laws are not in agreement with the Oglala Sioux Tribe Constitution. All decisions of the Supreme Court shall be in writing and shall be final.**
> **(c) Justices of the Supreme Court must have a Juris Doctorate from an A.B.A. accredited law school and must be licensed to practice law in any state or federal jurisdiction.**
> **(d) Justices of the Supreme Court shall be appointed to the Supreme Court by the Tribal council, and shall serve a six (6) year term.**

Section 4. Powers of the Inferior Tribal Court. The inferior tribal court shall exercise the following powers:

> **(a) Inferior tribal courts shall have the power to make findings of fact and conclusions of law, and shall have the power to issue all remedies in law and**

in equity including injunctive and declaratory relief and all writs including attachment and mandamus.

(b) Inferior tribal courts shall have the power to declare laws of the Oglala Sioux Tribe void if such laws are not in agreement with the Constitution.

(c) The Chief Judge of the inferior tribal courts shall oversee the administration of justice of inferior tribal courts and must have a Juris Doctorate from an A.B.A. accredited law school and must be licensed to practice law in any state or federal jurisdiction.

(d) The Chief Judge of inferior courts shall be elected at large by eligible voters of the Oglala Sioux Tribe under ordinances promulgated by the Tribal Council and shall serve a four (4) year term."

Section 5. "Compensation. The Tribal Council shall have the power to establish the level of compensation for Justices of the Supreme Court and Judges of inferior tribal courts, provided that compensation due to each Justice of Judge shall not be diminished during the Justice's or Judge's appointment.

Section 6. "Removal. The Tribal Council may remove any Justice of the Supreme Court or any Judge of inferior tribal courts by a two-thirds vote for:

(a) Unethical judicial conduct;

(b) Physical or mental disability with prevents the performance of judicial duties;

(c) Persistent failure to perform judicial duties;

(d) Gross misconduct that is clearly prejudicial to the administration of justice.

Section 7. "Vacancies. If there is any vacancy, the Tribal Council shall appoint a Justice of the Supreme Court or a new Judge of the inferior tribal courts for the unexpired term. If the vacancy involves the Chief Judge of the inferior tribal courts, the Tribal Council shall appoint a new Chief Judge for the unexpired term."

ARTICLE VI—DISTRICT ORGANIZATION

"Each district established under this constitution shall elect a president and such other officers as may be advisable to run concurrent with the terms of the representatives to the tribal council. The president shall call and preside over councils of the district whenever necessary for the consideration of matters of local interest. The various districts may consult with representatives of the Interior Department or the Superintendent or Commissioner of Indian Affairs, may undertake and manage local enterprises in furtherance of the purposes set forth in the preamble of this constitution, may levy assessments upon members of the district, may expend moneys in the district treasury for the benefit of the district, may keep a roll of those members of the tribe affiliated with the district, and may exercise such further powers as may be delegated to districts by the tribal council The actions of the district council shall not be inconsistent with the constitution and by-laws, and ordinances of the tribe.

ARTICLE VII—ELECTIONS

Section 1. All members of the Tribe 18 years of age or over, who have resided on the reservation for a period of one year immediately prior to any election shall have the right to vote.

Section 2. The time, place and manner of nomination and election of councilman and other elective officers of the council shall be determined by the tribal council by appropriate ordinances.

Section 3. The tribal council and officers shall be sworn into office the first meeting in December, commencing in 1998. The tribal council members elected in 1996 shall serve until the first meeting in December 1998.

ARTICLE VIII—REMOVAL OF OFFICERS

Section l. Any member or officer of the tribal council who is convicted of a felony or any other offense involving dishonesty shall forfeit his office.

Section 2. Any officer of the council or any councilman shall be subject to recall from office under due process of law for cause. Any complaint against any officer of the council or any councilman must be in writing and sworn to by the complainant. No person is to be impeached except by a two-thirds vote of the council after the accused has had due notice of the charges against him and an opportunity to be heard in his own defense.

ARTICLE IX—REFERENDUM

Section 1. Upon a petition by at least one-third (1/3) of the eligible voters of the Oglala Sioux Tribe, or upon the request of a majority of the members of the tribal council, any enacted or proposed ordinance or resolution of the council shall be submitted to popular referendum, and the vote of a majority of the qualified voters voting in such a referendum shall be conclusive and binding on the tribal council.

ARTICLE X—LAND

Section 1. Allotted lands—Allotted lands including heirship lands, within the Pine Ridge Indian Reservation, shall continue to be held as heretofore by their present owners. It is recognized that under existing law such lands may be inherited by the heirs of the present owner, whether or not, they are members of the Oglala Sioux Tribe. Likewise it is recognized that under existing law the Secretary of the Interior may, at his discretion, remove restrictions upon such land, upon application by the Indian owner, whereupon the land will become subject to State taxes and may be mortgaged or sold. The right of individual Indian to hold or to part with his land, as under existing law, shall not be abrogated by anything contained in this constitution, but the owner of restricted land may, with the approval of the Secretary of the Inferior, voluntarily convey his land to the Oglala Sioux Tribe either in exchange for a money payment or in exchange for an assignment covering the same land or other land as hereinafter provided.

Section 2. Tribal lands—The unallotted lands of the Pine Ridge Indian Reservation and all lands which may hereafter be acquired by the Oglala Sioux Tribe or by the United States in trust for the Oglala Sioux Tribe, shall be held as tribal lands, and no part of such land shall be mortgaged or sold. Tribal lands shall not be allotted to individual Indians but may be assigned to members of the Oglala Sioux Tribe, or leased, or otherwise used by the tribe, as hereinafter provided.

Section 3. Leasing of tribal lands—Tribal lands may be leased by the tribal council, with the approval of the Secretary the Interior for such periods of item as are permitted by law.

In the leasing of tribal lands preference shall be given, first to Indian communities or cooperative associations and, secondly to individual Indians who are members of the Oglala Sioux Tribe. No lease of tribal land to a nonmember shall be made by the tribal council unless it shall appear that no Indian community or cooperative associate or individual member of the tribe is able and willing to use the land and to pay a reasonable fee for such use. Grazing permits covering tribal land may be issued by the tribal council, with the approval of the Secretary of the Interior, in the same manner and upon the same terms of leases.

Section 4. Grant of standard assignments—In any assignment of tribal lands which are now owned by the tribe or which may be hereafter purchased for the tribe by the United States, or purchased by the tribe out of tribal funds, preference shall be given, first to the heads of families which have no allotted lands or interests in allotted lands but shall have already received assignments consisting of less than 20 acres agricultural land, or other land or interests in land of equal value.

No allotted member of the tribe who may hereafter have the restrictions upon his land removed and whose land may thereafter be alienated shall be entitled to receive an assignment of land as a landless Indian.

The tribal council may, if it sees fit, charge a fee of $10 on approval of an assignment made under this section. Assignments made under his section shall be for the primary purpose of establishing homes for landless Indians and shall be known as standard assignments.

Section 5. Tenure of standard assignments—If any member of the tribe holding a standard assignment of land shall, for a period of two years, fail to use the land so assigned or shall use such land for any unlawful purpose, his assignment may be cancelled by the tribal council after due notice and an opportunity to be heard and the said land may be reassigned in accordance with the provisions of Section 4 of this article.

Upon the death of any Indian holding a standard assignment, his heirs or other individuals designated by him, by will, or written request, shall have a preference in the reassignment of the land provided such persons are members of the Oglala Sioux Tribe who would be eligible to receive a standard assignment.

Section 6. Grant of exchange assignments—Any member of the tribe who owns an allotment or any share of heirship land or patent in fee land may voluntarily transfer his interest in such land to the tribe in exchange for an assignment to same land or land of equal value. If the assignee prefers, he may receive, in lieu of a specific tract of land, a proportionate share in a larger grazing unit.

Section 7. Leasing of exchange assignments—Exchange assignments may be used by the assignee or leased by him to Indian cooperative associates, to individual members of the tribe, or if no individual Indian or Indian cooperative association is able and willing to rent the land at a reasonable fee, such assignments may be leased to non-Indian, in the same manner as allotted lands.

Section 8. Inheritance of exchange assignments—Upon the death of the holder of an exchange assignment, such land shall be reassigned by the tribal council to his heirs or devisees, subject to the following conditions.

(a) Such lands may not be reassigned to any heir or devisee who is not a member of the Oglala Sioux Tribe, except that a life assignment may be made to the surviving widower, widow, or child of the holder of an assignment.

(b) Such lands may not be reassigned to any heir or devisee who already holds more than 1,280 acres of grazing land, or other land or interests in land of equal value, either under allotment or under assignment.

(c) Such lands may not be subdivided among heirs or devisees into units too small for convenient management. No area of grazing land shall be subdivided into units smaller than 160 acres, and no area of agricultural land shall be subdivided into unites smaller than two and one-half acres, except that land used for buildings or other improvements maybe divided to fit the convenience of the parties. Where it is impossible to divide the land properly among the eligible heirs or devisees, the tribal council shall issue to such heirs or devisees grazing permits or other interests in trial lands of the same value as the assignment of the decedent.

(d) If there are no eligible heirs or devisees of the decedent, the land shall be eligible for reassignment in accordance with the provisions of Section 4 of this article.

Section 9. Inheritance of improvements—Improvements of any character made upon lands may be bequeathed to and inherited by members of the Oglala Sioux Tribe under such regulations, as the tribal council shall provide. No permanent improvements shall be removed without the consent of the council.

Section 10. Exchange of assignments—Assignments may be exchanged between members of the Oglala Sioux Tribe by common consent in such manner, as the tribal council shall designate.

Section 11. Use of unassigned tribal land—Tribal land which is not leased or assigned, including tribal timber reserves, shall be managed by the tribal council for the benefit of the members of the entire tribe, and any cash income derived from such land shall accrue to the benefit of the tribe as a whole.

Section 12. Purchase of land by tribe—Tribal funds may be used with the consent of the Secretary of the Interior to acquire land under the following conditions.

(a) Land within the Pine Ridge Indian Reservation or adjacent to the boundaries thereof which is not now in Indian ownership may be purchased by or for the Oglala Sioux Tribe.

(b) Land owned by any member of the tribe who desires to leave the reservation permanently may be purchased by the tribe, under such terms as may be agreed upon.

Section 13. Method of making assignments—Applications for assignments shall be filed with the secretary of the tribal council and shall be in writing, setting forth the name of the person or persons applying for the land and as accurate a description of the land desired as the circumstances will permit. Notices of all applications received by the secretary shall be posted by him/her in the agency office and in at least three conspicuous places in the district in which the land is located for not less than 20 days before action is taken by the council. Any member of the tribe wishing to oppose the granting of an assignment shall do so in writing, setting forth his/her objections to be filed with the secretary of the tribal council, and may, if he/she so desires, appear before the council to present evidence. The secretary of the tribal council shall furnish the superintendent or other officer in charge of the agency a complete record of all action taken by the council on applications for assignment of land and a complete record of assignments shall be kept in the agency office and shall be open for inspection by members of the tribe.

ARTICLE XI—AMENDMENTS

This constitution and by-laws may be amended by a majority vote of the qualified voters of the tribe voting at an election called for the purpose by the Secretary of the Interior, provided that at least thirty (30) percent of those entitled to vote shall vote in such election; but no amendment shall become effective until it shall have been approved by the Secretary of the Interior. It shall be the duty of the Secretary of the Interior to call an election on any proposed amendment, at the request of two-thirds (2/3) of the council, or upon presentation of a petition signed by one-third (1/3) of the qualified voters, members of the tribe.

ARTICLE XII—BILL OF RIGHTS

The Tribal Council in exercising its inherent powers of self-government, shall not make any tribal law or enforce any tribal, state or federal law that:

(a) Prohibits the full exercise of Lakota culture and spirituality or any other religion or abridging the freedom of speech, or of the press, or the right of the people to peacefully assemble and to petition for a redress of grievances.

(b) Violates the right of the people to be secure in their persons, houses, papers, and effects against unreasonable search and seizures; nor issue warrants, but upon probable cause, supported by oath or affirmation, and particularly describing the place to be searched and the person or thing to be seized;

(c) Subjects any person for the same offense to be twice put in jeopardy;

(d) Compels any person in any criminal case to be a witness against himself or herself;

(e) Takes any private property for public use without just compensation;

(f) Denies to any person in a criminal proceeding the right to a speedy and public trial, to be informed of the nature and cause of the accusation, to be confronted with witnesses against the person, to have compulsory process for obtaining witnesses in the person's favor, and at the person's own expense, to have the assistance of counsel for the person's defense;

(g) Requires excessive bail, impose excessive fines, inflicts cruel and unusual punishments;

(h) Denies to any person within its jurisdiction the equal protection of its laws or deprives any person of liberty or property without due process of law;

(i) Adopts any bill of attainder or ex post facto law; or

(j) Denies to any person accused of an offense punishable by imprisonment the right, upon request, to a trial by jury of not less than six (6) persons.

ARTICLE XIII—RESPONSIBILITIES OF EXECUTIVE COMMITTEE OFFICERS

Section 1. It shall be the duty of the president to preside over all meetings of the Oglala Sioux Tribal Council and to carry out all orders of the council, unless prevented by just causes. The President, with the assistance of subordinate Executive Committee Officers, shall also exercise powers delegated to the President by the Tribal Council.

Section 2. The vice president shall perform the duties and execute the powers of the president in the absence of the president and shall assume the presidency in the event of a vacancy in the office.

Section 3. The Secretary shall keep an official record of each regular and special meetings of the tribal council, meetings of sub-committees of the Tribal Council, and meetings of the Executive Committee, and shall perform such other duties delegated to the Secretary by the Tribal Council. The Secretary shall make available to the public all laws, rules, regulations, and meeting minutes adopted by the Tribal Council and the Executive Committee.

Section 4. The Treasurer shall be the custodian of all moneys, which come under the jurisdiction, or control of the Oglala Sioux Tribal Council. He shall pay out funds in accordance with the laws established by the Tribal Council, shall keep accounts of all receipts and disbursements, and shall make written report to the Tribal Council at each Regular and Special meeting. The Treasurer shall be bonded in such an amount the Tribal Council by law shall provide. The books of the Treasurer shall be subject to inspection or audit by the direction of the Tribal Council.

Section 5. The Fifth Member shall inform the Executive Committee of the actions taken by the Tribal Council and shall report back to the Tribal Council the actions or implementations taken by the executive Committee. The Tribal Council may also assign other duties to the Fifth Member.

Section 6. There shall be an Executive Committee, which shall consist of the President, the Vice President, the Secretary, the Treasurer, and the Fifth Member. The Executive Committee shall act on behalf of the Tribal Council when the Tribal Council is not in session and shall have charge of all routine matters which shall arise during such recess, including the administration of the land provisions of this constitution, and such other matters as may be delegated to it by the Tribal Council, and shall adopt resolutions that are not inconsistent with resolutions or ordinances adopted by the Tribal Council.

ARTICLE XIV—QUALIFICAITONS OF TRIBAL COUNCIL REPRESENTATIVES AND EXECUTIVE COMMITTEE OFFICERS

Any person elected as a Tribal Council Representative or as a Executive Committee Officer must be a member of the Oglala Sioux Tribe, be at least thirty (30) years of age at the time of the election, and must reside within the exterior boundaries of the Pine Ridge Indian Reservation as defined in Article I

ARTICLE XV—OATH OF OFFICE

Section 1. Each Tribal Council Representative and Executive Committee Officer shall be required to take an oath of office prior to assuming constitutional duties.

(Oath) I, _____ do solemnly swear that I will promote, preserve, and strengthen the general health and welfare of the Oglala Lakota Oyate; and I will support and defend this Constitution and the human rights of the Oglala Lakota Oyate and the human rights of other peoples as recognized in international laws, and treaties which includes both the 1851 and 1868 Fort Laramie Treaties and, declarations.

ARTICLE XVI—MEETINGS AND PROCEDURES

Section 1. The Oglala Sioux Tribal Council shall conduct a mandatory Regular meeting on the last Tuesday of each month, but if the last Tuesday of each month falls on any holiday officially observed by the Oglala Sioux Tribe, the Regular meeting shall occur on the next business day.

Section 2. Two-thirds (2/3) of the duly elected members must be present to constitute a quorum.

Section 3. When a majority of Tribal Council members sign a written statement requesting a Special meeting, the President shall call a Special meeting no sooner than two (2) days.

Section 4. The Tribal Council may adopt an Ordinance establishing the process for the President to call emergency meetings to deal with natural, biological or chemical disasters.

Section 5. The Tribal Council shall adopt an Ordinance establishing the order of business in any regular or special meeting.

ARTICLE XVII—NATIONAL SIOUX COUNCIL

The tribal council may appoint delegates to represent the Oglala Sioux Tribe in National Sioux Councils.

BYLAWS OF THE
OGLALA SIOUX TRIBE

ARTICLE IV—SALARIES

Section 1. The salaries and expense payments of the councilmen and other officers of the Oglala Sioux Tribe may be paid out of available funds of the tribe in accordance with ordinances duly enacted, provided that no council shall enact any ordinance increasing the salaries or per diem expense payments of councilmen during the existing term of office.

Section 2. No compensation shall be paid to any councilman, president, vice-president, secretary, treasurer, tribal council, or any officer out of tribal funds under the control of the Federal Government, except upon a resolution stating the amount of compensation and the nature of services approved by the Secretary of the Interior.

ARTICLE VII—ADOPOTION OF CONSTITUTON AND BYLAWS

Section 1. This constitution and the attached Bylaws when approved by a majority of the adult voters of the Oglala Sioux Tribe voting in a special election called by the Secretary of the Interior in which at least thirty (30) per cent of the eligible voters vote, shall be submitted to the Secretary of the Interior for approval and shall be effective from the date of such approval.

CERTIFICATE OF ADOPTION

Pursuant to an order, approved December 11, 1935, by the Secretary of the Interior, the attached constitution and by-laws was submitted for ratification to the members of the Oglala Sioux Tribe of Indians of the Pine Ridge Reservation and was on December 14, 1935, duly approved by a vote of 1,348 for, and 1,041 against, in an election in which over 30 percent of those entitled to vote cast their ballots, in accordance with Section 16 of the Indian Reorganization Act of June 18, 1934 (48 Stat. 984), as amended by the Act of June 15, 1935 (Pub. No. 147, 74th Cong.).

William Fire Thunder, Chairman of Election Board

William Pugh, Secretary of Election Board

James H. McGregor, Superintendent in Charge of Reservation

Commentary: The constitution of the Oglala Sioux Tribe was first adopted in 1935. It was amended in 1969, 1985, 1997, and in 2008. The 2008 amendments include the Bill of Rights, which is unique to most tribal constitutions. The 2008 amendments also empowered the tribal courts with jurisdiction to declare laws of the Oglala Sioux Tribe void if they are in conflict with the constitution. The latter amendment is consistent with the tribal members' vote for a separation of powers mandate which establishes a balance of power between the legislative, the executive, and the judicial branches of government.

The United States Constitution does not provide authority for the U.S. Supreme Court to declare laws unconstitutional. The power of the Supreme Court to declare laws unconstitutional was assumed by Chief Justice John Marshall in 1803 in the case of *Marbury v. Madison,* 1 Cranch 137; 2. Ed. 60 (1803). Congress attempted to expand the original jurisdiction of the Supreme Court to issue writs of mandamus, a power that was not provided in Article III of the Constitution. The Supreme Court's original jurisdiction is limited, and Congress does not have the authority to amend the Constitution. This decision resulted in the U.S. Supreme Court's authority to require laws to be in compliance with the Constitution; and if a law is in conflict with the Constitution, the Supreme Court may declare the law to be unconstitutional and therefore void and unenforceable.

The tribal constitution is unique in that it specifically grants jurisdiction to the lower tribal court, and the Tribal Supreme Court, to declare laws of the tribal council void for failure to comply with the tribal constitution.

CHAPTER EIGHT

CRIMINAL JURISDICTION

A basic definition of jurisdiction is the authority of a court to hear and decide a case. There are several levels of jurisdiction that require further analysis, including subject matter jurisdiction, personal jurisdiction, and territorial jurisdiction. Differences in jurisdiction include those of criminal jurisdiction and civil jurisdiction. A case is first filed in a court of original jurisdiction. If one of the parties disagrees with the decision made by a court of original jurisdiction, then that party might appeal to an appellate court (usually a federal court of appeals) or, eventually, to the Supreme Court. Tribal courts consist of a court of original jurisdiction where trials are held, as well as a tribal Supreme Court where lower court decisions are reviewed for their legality. These jurisdictional areas are frequently addressed when deciding whether a tribal court has jurisdiction. Tribal courts are faced with decisions of the U.S. Supreme Court, which has heard and decided many cases involving the extent of tribal jurisdiction.

Leading cases on Criminal Jurisdiction in Indian Country.

Ex Parte Crow Dog, 109 U.S. 556 (1883)

One of the earliest criminal cases involving an Indian tribe was the Crow Dog case. Crow Dog killed Spotted Tail on the Rosebud Agency of the Great Sioux Reservation in 1881. The Federal District Court for Dakota Territory convicted Crow Dog and imposed a death sentence to be carried out in January 1884. The Supreme Court reversed the conviction after deciding that the federal courts did not have criminal jurisdiction over Indians who commit crimes against other Indians of the same band. The Brule' tribal council had resolved the case after hearing from the Spotted Tail family members and Crow Dog. The parties agreed that Crow Dog would make restitution to the family by paying $600, eight horses, and a blanket, rather than enact retribution. The tribal council was enforcing custom law of the Sioux, which was a peacemaking process. The BIA officials had initiated an attempt to acquire federal jurisdiction over crimes committed by Indians on the reservation as a part of the assimilation policies of the federal government.

Two years later, Congress enacted the Major Crimes Act, which provides federal jurisdiction over felonies committed by Indians on the reservations.

United States v. McBratney, 104 U.S. 621 (1882)

McBratney was a white man who killed another white man on the Ute Reservation in Colorado. McBratney was indicted and convicted in the United States Court for the District of Colorado. On appeal, the U.S. Supreme Court ruled that McBratney was subject to state law. The Court decided that state law applies to criminal acts committed by a non-Indian against another non-Indian even though the crime was committed on the reservation. The Court's rationale for the decision is based on the fact that Colorado was admitted into the Union on "equal footing" with the original states. The original states were given criminal jurisdiction over white citizens who commit crimes within its borders, and since Colorado was admitted into the Union on equal footing with the original states, then Colorado (or the state) has jurisdiction over crimes committed by non-Indians against other non-Indians on Indian reservations. This is a prime example of an activist court; in this case, the Supreme Court was involved in making a law, which is normally made by the legislative branch of government, or Congress. Even so, the law has been accepted by the United States, and this court-made law still prevails in Indian country.

United States v. Antelope, 430 U.S. 641. (1977)

Gabriel Francis Antelope, the Defendant, was arrested on the Coeur d'Alene Indian Reservation and was charged with federal crimes of burglary, robbery, and murder under the Major Crimes Act. The Defendant and his accomplices were in the process of burglarizing the home of an elderly 81-year-old white woman, Emma Johnson. During burglary and robbery, Mrs. Johnson died at the crime scene. The facts do not establish the cause of her death; Antelope and his accomplices were convicted and were sentenced under the federal felony murder statute. The federal court concluded that Antelope was guilty of first-degree murder under the felony murder statute that applies to federal crimes. The felony murder rule provides that if death occurs during the commission of a crime, then the perpetrator is guilty of first-degree murder. The U. S. Attorney does not have to establish premeditation as an element of first-degree murder. On appeal, the U.S. Court of Appeals for the Ninth Circuit concluded that under Idaho State law, the state would have to prove premeditation as a condition of first-degree murder, which requires that a defendant act with the purpose of causing the death of the decedent. Because the state law differed so greatly from the federal law, the Court of Appeals ruled that Antelope was "put at a serious racially-based disadvantage". On appeal to the U.S. Supreme Court, the court reversed the decision of the Court of Appeals. The high court ruled that the

Major Crimes Act, which applies only to Indians "is not based on impermissible racial classifications. Quite the contrary, classification expressly singling out Indian tribes as subjects of legislation are expressly provided for in the Constitution and supported by the ensuing history of the Federal Government's relations with Indians."

Antelope represents a case that does not directly promote Indian interests in federal legislation, such as the Indian Preference statute of the Indian Reorganization Act. Article I of the U.S. Constitution empowers Congress with the authority to regulate commerce with Indian tribes, and consequently enacts laws that apply only to Indians. Most Indian laws favor Indian interests, but there are some that put Indians at a disadvantage, such as the Major Crimes Act. The high court stated that "Indeed, respondents were not subjected to federal criminal jurisdiction because they are of the Indian race, but because they were enrolled members of the Coeur d'Alene Tribe. We therefore conclude that federal criminal statutes enforced here are based neither in whole nor in part upon impermissible racial classifications." There are many references to the "unique legal status" of Indians, which characterize Indians as a separate class of citizens under the Constitution.

It is very important for tribal members to understand that Indian laws apply only to Indians and that the Supreme Court has upheld such laws when challenged by non-Indians. A prime example is the case in which the Supreme Court upheld Indian Preference as applying only to Indians and describing how it does not discriminate against non-Indians. The case, *Morton v. Mancari*, 417 U. S. 535 (1974), clarifies the Indian Preference statute as the prevailing Indian policy of the Bureau of Indian Affairs. In that case, the Secretary of the Interior decided to extend Indian Preference to promotions for Indians who were already employed within the BIA. Until then, the preference had been limited to initial hiring, where Indians were given preference in selections for BIA jobs. A group of non-Indian BIA employees in the Albuquerque Area Office challenged the legality of Indian Preference. They argued that extending preferences to Indians was in violation of the 1972 Equal Employment Opportunity Act, and that it denied them due process and equal protection of law. The U. S. District Court for the District of New Mexico ruled in Mancari's favor, holding that the Indian Preference statute was repealed by the 1972 Act because it extended "racial" preference to Indians who were qualified for employment in the BIA. The Supreme Court, however, reversed the lower court's decision. The Supreme Court quoted Senator Humphrey, who explained that the Equal Employment Opportunity Act of 1972 prohibited discrimination in private employment based on "race, color, religion, sex, or national origin." Senator Humphrey cited an exemption from its coverage applicable to the preferential employment of Indians by Indian tribes or by industries located on or near Indian reservations. Senator Humphrey stated "This exemption is consistent with the Federal Government's policy of encouraging Indian employment and with the special legal position of Indians." 110 Cong. Rec. 12723 (1964).

The Court cited other reasons for upholding the Indian Preference Statute and the extension of Indian preference to promotions as well as initial hiring. In addition to the exceptions made for tribal employment, the Court cited the Educational Amendments of 1972, which required the Government to give preference to Indians in the training of teachers of Indian children. The Educational Amendments of 1972 provided federal funds to colleges and universities to be used in the training of Indian teachers. The policy of the government was to provide Indian teachers for Indian students in reservation schools. As a result, many colleges established satellite campuses on various Indian reservations. Black Hills State University began offering classes at Pine Ridge in the early 70's, and the tribe's Higher Education Learning Center came into existence. It has since been named Oglala Community College, and is presently known as Oglala Lakota College. Other reservations had similar experiences, and continue to provide higher education learning opportunities to tribal members. Sicangu University is operated on the Rosebud Sioux Reservation; Sitting Bull College operates on the Standing Rock Sioux Reservation; Big Foot College was established on the Cheyenne River Indian Reservation. The colleges eventually became independent of the sponsoring college or university, and now receive annual funding under the Public Law 474, Indian Community College Act.

The Indian Community College Act represents another law that is uniquely "Indian", in that funding is made directly to Native American colleges based on enrollment of tribal members. Indian laws such as these make up a total volume of the Federal Code. Title 25 of the Federal Code is designated as a title devoted entirely to legislation on the subject of "Indians".

OLIPHANT v. SUQUAMISH INDIAN TRIBE, 435 U.S. 191 (1978)

While making laws on the subject of Indians is constitutionally committed strictly to Congress as the legislative branch of government, there are times when the Supreme Court will actively engage in lawmaking for Indian tribes. *Oliphant* is a classic example of a court-made law that is totally without merit, and is an affront to Indian nations. Indian nations historically enjoyed their inherent right to govern themselves, and to exercise sovereign powers that were inherent by virtue of their status as independent nations. The case, *Oliphant v. Suquamish Indian Tribe* began when two white men, who were residents of the Port Madison Indian reservation near Seattle, Washington, were involved in a high-speed chase with the tribal police of that reservation. The men were charged with assaulting tribal police officers, resisting arrest, and damaging a tribal police vehicle. The Suquamish Tribal Court assumed jurisdiction of the case because it occurred on the reservation, and their laws extended to any person who violates tribal laws on the reservation. The defendants moved to dismiss the charges on grounds that the tribe lacked criminal jurisdiction over non-Indians. The U.S. District Court for the Western District of

Washington denied the appeal, and the Court of Appeals for the Ninth Circuit affirmed. The lower courts found that the "power to preserve order on the reservation . . . is a *sine qua non* (essential part) of the sovereignty that the Suquamish originally possessed." 544 F. 2d 1007, (1976)

Justice William Rehnquist delivered the opinion of the Court. The Court rejected the tribe's argument that its criminal jurisdiction over all persons within its jurisdiction flows automatically from the "Tribe's retained inherent powers of government over the Port Madison Indian Reservation." Justice Rehnquist ruled that Indian tribes do not have the inherent authority to impose its laws on non-Indians, and that the power to try and punish non-Indians for reservation crimes must be affirmatively conferred by Congress. The Court referred to an 1830 treaty with the Choctaw Indian Tribe wherein the Tribe was guaranteed "the jurisdiction and government of all the persons and property that may be within their limits. "However, the Choctaws "express a wish that Congress may grant to the Choctaws the right of punishing by their own laws any white man who shall come into their nation, and infringe any of their national regulations." Justice Rehnquist and the court used this reference to the Choctaw tribe from some one hundred and forty-eight years earlier to conclude that the Suquamish did not have the inherent authority to prosecute non-Indian offenders who commit crimes on the Port Madison Reservation. The fact that the Choctaws requested authority to prosecute non-Indian offenders was used as an excuse to deprive the Suquamish and other Indian tribes the ability to exercise their authority that is inherently within tribal government. The Court treated the Choctaws and the Suquamish as the same tribe, and enacted a federal law that applies to all Indian tribes.

The term "inherent" is defined in Webster's Dictionary as "existing in someone or something as a natural and inseparable quality, characteristic or right; innate; basic; inborn". Indian nations historically enforced their laws against all persons who happened to be in their territories. This practice dates back to the very beginning of Indian nations. At the time, there was no one to question whether native nations could or should enforce their customs and manage their territories as sovereign nations. No one ever said that once the United States establishes Congress, it takes Congress to allow Indian governments to enforce Indian laws on the reservation. The very notion that Congress must confer that power on Indian tribes is fiction, and Justice Rehnquist pointed to no law that Congress had divested the Suquamish Tribe of its inherent right to govern itself.

Chief Justice Berger and Associate Justice Thurgood Marshall disagreed with Rehnquist and the majority. Justice Marshall wrote his dissent, saying "I agree with the court below that the power to preserve order on the reservation is a *sine qua non* of the sovereignty that the Suquamish originally possessed. In the absence of affirmative withdrawal by treaty or statute, I am of the view that Indian tribes enjoy as a necessary aspect of their retained sovereignty the right to try and punish all persons who commit offenses against tribal law within the reservation. Accordingly, I dissent." (*Sine qua non* is Latin for "without which not" meaning that tribal sovereignty may not exist without tribal jurisdiction to enforce its laws on its land.)

Justices Berger and Marshall recognized the inherent right of Indian tribes to govern themselves, and that if that right had not been given up by treaty or federal law, it logically remains. The *Oliphant* decision is the result of an activist court that exercised legislative powers specifically reserved for Congress in the Constitution.

The decision creates chaos on Indian reservations, where white offenders go unpunished for crimes against Indians. In the case of misdemeanor offenses committed by non-Indians, the state has no jurisdiction to prosecute these cases, because the offenses occur on the reservation where the state lacks jurisdiction. The federal courts do not prosecute misdemeanors by non-Indians on the reservation, because the federal dockets are generally loaded with felony cases. The only remedy an Indian tribe has to deal with non-Indian criminals on the reservation is to exclude them from the reservation. This results in reservation crimes going unpunished, and Indian victims being denied justice simply because the Supreme Court exercised legislative powers of the Congress in violation of the Constitution.

Ironically, two years later, when a majority of the Supreme Court upheld the decision of the Court of Claims awarding the Sioux Nation $17.1 million for the unconstitutional taking of the Black Hills, Justice Rehnquist dissented because Congress referred the case to the Court of Claims for further review after the award of interest on the judgment had been denied. Justice Rehnquist adamantly criticized Congress for exercising judicial powers by referring the case back to the Court of Claims. Justice Rehnquist stated:

> "Although the Court refrains from so boldly characterizing its action, it is obvious from these facts that Congress has reviewed the decisions of the Court of Claims, set aside the judgment that no taking of the Black Hills occurred, set aside the judgment that here is no cognizable reason for relitigating this claim, and ordered a new trial. I am convinced that this is nothing other than an exercise of judicial power reserved to Art. III courts that may not be performed by the Legislative Branch under its Art. I authority. Article III vests "the judicial power of the United States" in federal courts. Congress is vested with *legislative* powers, and may not itself exercise an appellate-type review of judicial judgments in order to alter their terms, or to order new trials of cases already decided . . ."

United States v. Sioux Nation of Indians, 448 U.S. 371 (1980)

Justice Rehnquist ignored this constitutional distinction between the legislative function and the judicial function of government by drafting a Supreme Court Opinion that effectively legislated a law depriving Indian tribes of their basic, innate, inherent authority to enforce criminal laws over non-Indian lawbreakers on their reservations.

Justice Rehnquist was correct in that Congress is the proper branch of government to legislate matters involving Indian Tribes pursuant to Article I of the Constitution. However, he conveniently ignored this fundamental law, and judicially exercised legislative powers of Article 1 by legislating matters involving Indian tribes. Thus, Justice Rehnquist and those who joined him were "bad men among the whites" described in Article 1 of the Fort Laramie Treaty of 1868 for having stripped Indian tribes of their inherent authority to enforce their criminal laws against non-Indian lawbreakers on the reservations.

UNITED STATES V. MARCYES, U.S. Court of Appeals, Ninth Circuit 557 f. 2d 1861 (1977)

Marcyes is the leading case interpreting the Assimilated Crimes Act, which applies to Indian reservations. This federal law incorporates state law into the federal system, and applies it on the reservation as though it were a reservation crime. The Assimilative Crimes Act reads as follows:

"Whoever within or upon any of the places now existing or hereafter reserved or acquired as provided in section 7 of this title, is guilty of any act or omission which, although not made punishable by any enactment Congress, would be punishable if committed or omitted within the jurisdiction of the State, Territory, Possession, or District in which such place is situated, by the laws there of in force at the time of such act or omission, shall be guilty of a like offense and subject to a like punishment."

Marcyes was a member of the Puyallup Indian Reservation, located in East Tacoma, Washington. In June of 1975, Marcyes and others were operating a fireworks stand on the reservation. Washington State law prohibits fireworks. The federal authorities arrested them, and they were prosecuted in federal court for violating a state law. This is a very unusual kind of case, because neither federal law nor tribal law forbids the prohibited conduct. The conduct is forbidden by state law, and state law generally does not apply on Indian reservations. The law is designed to fill the gaps, which exist between state and federal law involving conduct that is not regulated by federal law. State jurisdiction is not involved; however, federal prosecutors who prosecute under the Assimilative Crimes Act enforce the state law in federal court. In other words, the federal law "assimilates" the state law into the federal scheme.

The Assimilative Crimes Act does not apply to activities that are lawfully regulated by tribal governments. For example, a bingo operation on the reservation may exceed the maximum payouts allowed by state bingo regulations, and the tribal regulations are permissible under federal law.

UNITED STATES V. WHEELER, Supreme Court of the United States, 1978. 435 U.S. 313.

The Indian defendant in this case entered a plea of guilty in Navajo Tribal Court to disorderly conduct, and to contributing to the delinquency of a minor. The defendant had sexual relations with a minor, and a year later the federal court indicted him and charged him with rape under the Major Crimes Act. The defendant raised the issue of double jeopardy because he had been charged in tribal court for the same incident. The Supreme Court ruled that double jeopardy does not apply to cases involving a tribal prosecution followed by a federal prosecution. The reasoning of the Supreme Court is that each prosecution is made by a separate sovereign power and each sovereign power is enforcing its own laws; thus, tribal prosecution does not count as a federal prosecution. The court found that the powers to enforce laws are derived from separate sources. The United States derives its power from the U.S. Constitution, and are distinguished from "The powers of Indian tribes that are, in general "*inherent powers of a limited sovereignty which has never been extinguished.*"—F. Cohen, Handbook of Federal Indian Law 122 (1945) The court concluded that "It is evident that the sovereign power to punish tribal offenders has never been given up by the Navajo Tribe and that tribal exercise of that power today is therefore the continued exercise of retained tribal sovereignty . . ."

Consequently, if one is prosecuted in tribal court for an offense that also qualifies as a federal offense, both governments can legally prosecute the offender. Each government derives its power from a separate source and they do not exercise each other's criminal jurisdiction.

STATE OF SOUTH DAKOTA v. PETER SPOTTED HORSE, (Citation omitted) Supreme Court of South Dakota, October 4, 1990.

The Defendant, Peter Spotted Horse, was a member of the Standing Rock Sioux Tribe. On April 1, 1988, he was observed driving a motor vehicle in Mobridge, SD, which is off the reservation. Since he was not displaying valid 1988 license plate stickers, the Mobridge City Police officer attempted to pull him over for a traffic citation. Spotted

Horse refused to stop, and instead, drove across the Missouri River bridge onto the Standing Rock Sioux Reservation. The city police officer pursued him with his red lights flashing, and continued to pursue him onto the reservation. Spotted Horse turned off the highway and drove within the city limits of a small reservation town of Wakpala. Spotted Horse drove onto the driveway of his home and the city police officer parked behind him. The officer approached the vehicle and attempted to remove Spotted Horse from the vehicle. When Spotted Horse refused to exit the vehicle, the office beat him with his nightstick and pulled him out of the car by his arms. He then threw him to the ground and pinned him with his knee to his back and handcuffed him. He then put him in the squad car and drove him back to Mobridge, where he lodged Spotted Horse in the city jail.

While driving to Mobridge, the officer detected the smell of alcohol on Spotted Horse. He administered a field sobriety test, which Sported Horse failed. A blood test was taken and the results of the BAC were 0.244. Spotted Horse was charged with (1) eluding police in violation of state law, (2) driving while under the influence of alcohol, (3) resisting arrest, (4) driving without a license and (5) failure to display current registration of a motor vehicle. The trial court acquitted Spotted Horse of counts 1 and 3, eluding and resisting arrest. The fourth charge, driving without a license, was dismissed during trial. He was convicted of counts 2 and 5, driving under the influence and failure to display current registration. Spotted Horse appealed to the Supreme Court of South Dakota arguing that the state lacked "jurisdiction to try an Indian who committed a misdemeanor off the reservation but who fled to the reservation and was arrested by a municipal police officer on the reservation."

The court found that South Dakota is a disclaimer state—that is, one which disclaimed jurisdiction over Indian reservations as a condition of statehood, and that the state had not accepted jurisdiction as it could have under Public Law 280, which allowed disclaimer states to amend their constitutions and assume jurisdiction over Indian reservations. The state could have unilaterally assumed jurisdiction over Indian reservations between the years, 1953 through 1968, when the law was amended to require tribal consent before any state may assume jurisdiction over Indian reservations. The high court reversed Spotted Horse's conviction of driving under the influence because the city police officer had no authority to arrest an Indian on the reservation, where the violation was first discovered. The court stated that the state police officer's actions in pursuing Spotted Horse onto the reservation to be a constitutional violation because the state constitution prohibits enforcement of state laws on the reservation by state authorities. The only charge that survived appeal was the failure to display current registration tags on his vehicle. That offense was committed in the town of Mobridge, which the city police officer first observed. The alcohol offense was discovered by the city police officer while making an illegal arrest and the evidence was not admissible in the state court. The Court also stated that the city police officer could have, and should have, notified the tribal police when he discovered that Spotted Horse was under the influence. The tribal court had jurisdiction over Spotted Horse while he was on the reservation, and driving under the influence is a tribal offense, which would be prosecuted by tribal prosecutors in tribal court.

This case stands for the rule that there is no right of hot pursuit from state jurisdiction onto tribal jurisdiction. A state police officer pursuing a tribal member onto the reservation loses jurisdiction by crossing the boundaries of the reservation. Once he takes that action, the only authority he has is to call the tribal police if he has probable cause to believe the driver is violating tribal law. This case was reaffirmed in a later case involving member of the Oglala Sioux Tribe, Nick Cummings, who was pursued onto the Pine Ridge Reservation by a state highway patrol officer and was lodged in Fall River County jail at Hot Springs, South Dakota. The South Dakota State Supreme Court ruled that there was no fresh pursuit agreement between the state and the tribe, and that state police officers do not have the right to pursue tribal members onto the reservation.

VIOLENCE AGAINST WOMEN ACT (VAWA). On March 14, 2013, President Barack Obama signed an amendment to the Violence Against Women Act, which extends tribal jurisdiction to cases of domestic violence committed by non-Indians against Indian women. The law will not take effect until 2015. In the meantime, the tribes must amend their criminal codes to accommodate the new federal law so that the non-Indian defendants are provided the basic constitutional rights that they would otherwise enjoy as American citizens.

CHAPTER NINE

CIVIL JURISDICTION

WILLIAMS v. LEE, Supreme Court of the United States, 1959. 358 U.S. 217.

The owner of a trading post on the Navajo Reservation brought suit against the Navajo tribal member for the collection of goods sold on credit. The transactions took place on the reservation, but the non-Indian owner of the trading post filed his lawsuit in the Superior Court of Arizona. The tribal member filed a motion to dismiss the case, alleging that jurisdiction of the case was in the tribal court rather than in the state court. The lower court and Supreme Court of Arizona ruled in favor of state jurisdiction. The decision was based on the fact that there was no act of Congress which specifically prohibited the state court to hear cases filed by non-Indians against Indians, and that the state was free to exercise its jurisdiction over the case. On appeal, the United States Supreme Court reversed and upheld tribal jurisdiction over civil actions that arise on Indian reservations. In the court's opinion, "Essentially, absent governing Acts of Congress, the question has always been whether the state action infringed on the right of reservation Indians to make their own laws and be ruled by them."

The Court elaborated on the relationship between the government and the Navajo Tribe, which was amplified in the treaty between the United States and the Navajo Nation of June 1, 1868. The treaty "set apart" for "their permanent home" a portion of what had been their native country, and provided that no one, except the United Sates Government personnel, was to enter the reserved area. The Court went on to say that "Congress has also acted consistently upon the assumption that the States have no power to regulate the affairs of Indians on a reservation . . . Significantly, when Congress has wished the States to exercise this power, it has expressly granted them the jurisdiction, which *Worcester v. Georgia* had denied . . . "No Federal Act has given state courts jurisdiction over such controversies."

In expressing the importance of Indian tribes to govern themselves, the Court further stated "There can be no doubt that to allow the exercise of state jurisdiction here would undermine the authority of tribal courts over Reservation affairs and hence would infringe on the right of the Indians to govern themselves."

The Court referred to the earlier, 1832 case, *Worcester v. Georgia*, 31 U.S. 515, which held that the State of Georgia had no jurisdiction to enforce any of its laws on the Cherokee Reservation. Despite this ruling that was the accepted standard of law involving state jurisdiction on Indian reservations, the State of Arizona, it seems, was a slow learner. Two more Arizona cases followed the *Williams* case involving the issue of state jurisdiction on Indian land. Arizona lost these two cases at the U.S. Supreme Court level.

WARREN TRADING POST CO. v. ARIZONA TAX COMMISSION, United States Supreme Court, 380 U.S. 685 (1965)

This case involves another white trader who operated a trading post on the Navajo Reservation. The Arizona Tax Commission levied a 2% tax on the "gross proceeds of sales, or gross income" from sales made on the reservation. The Trading Post operated on the reservation under a license granted by the Bureau of Indian Affairs. A challenge to state authority to tax reservation sales was denied by the Supreme Court of Arizona. On appeal to the U.S. Supreme Court, the court reversed the decision of the Arizona court and declared that Congress and the tribe itself regulate Indian trade exclusively. The court reasoned that the all-inclusive regulations and federal laws governing Indian traders "show that Congress has taken the business of Indian trading on reservations so fully in hand that no room remains for state laws imposing additional burdens upon traders."

This case stands for the fact that states may not impose taxes on sales made by traders on reservations, although there are some exceptions. One notable exception is the so-called sales tax that is imposed on sales made by retailers on the Pine Ridge Reservation. The Oglala Sioux Tribe and the South Dakota Department of Revenue have had a sales tax agreement in place for many years. The retailers add a sales tax to sales, which is called a state sales tax. This tax is collected and submitted to the SD Department of Revenue. At the end of each year, the Department of Revenue rebates approximately 90% of the revenue back to the Tribe for its use. Theoretically, the sales tax is a tribal tax that is collected by the state and paid back to the tribe at the end of the year, minus an administrative collection fee.

McCLANAHAN v. ARIZONA STATE TAX COMMISSION, Supreme Court of the United States, (1973) 411 U.S. 164

The State of Arizona again tried to impose a tax on a Navajo tribal member, Rosalind McClanahan, who worked on the Navajo reservation. Her employer withheld $16.20 from her wages earned during the year to cover her obligation to pay state income taxes. She filed her state income tax return and paid the tax under protest and claimed a refund arguing that the state had no right to collect a state income tax from her earnings on the reservation. There was no response so she filed in Arizona Superior Court. The lower court and the Arizona Court of Appeals dismissed her case and held that the state income tax does not infringe on the right of the Navajo tribe to be self-governing.

On appeal to the United States Supreme Court, Arizona lost again. The high court noted, "The policy of leaving Indians free from state jurisdiction and control is deeply rooted in the Nation's history." The Court cited the Arizona Enabling Act, which was used by the Territory of Arizona to achieve statehood. Under the Enabling Act, the Territory must submit its proposed state constitution to Congress for approval before it could enter the Union as one of the United States. Statehood was expressly conditioned upon the promise that the State would "forever disclaim all right and title to all lands lying within said boundaries owned or held by any Indian or Indian tribes, the right or title to which shall have been acquired through or from the United States or any prior sovereign, and that until the title of such Indian or Indian tribes shall have been extinguished the same shall be and remain subject to the disposition and under the absolute jurisdiction and control of the Congress of the United Sates"—Arizona Enabling Act, 36 Stat. 569. The Court further elaborated by quoting "Nor is the Arizona Enabling Act silent on the specific question of tax immunity. The Act expressly provides that "nothing herein, or in the ordinance herein provided for, shall preclude the said State from taxing as other lands and other property are taxed any lands and other property *outside of an Indian reservation* owned or held by any Indian."

The Arizona State Constitution prohibited state taxation on any reservation Indian, and in that sense the State of Arizona was in violation of its own constitution by assessing an income tax on the tribal member in this case. The Court also cited Public Law 280, which allowed states with disclaimers in their constitutions to amend their constitutions and to assume jurisdiction over Indian reservations.

The Court emphasized the weakness of the Arizona case by stating, "Arizona, of course, has neither amended its constitution to permit taxation of the Navajos nor secured the consent of the Indians affected. Indeed, a startling aspect of this case is that the appellee (Arizona) apparently concedes that, in the absence of compliance with 25

U.S.C.A. 1322(a)—(P.L. 280,) the Arizona courts can exercise neither civil nor criminal jurisdiction over reservation Indians. But the appellee nowhere explains how without such jurisdiction the State's tax may either be imposed or collected. Unless the State is willing to defend the position that it may constitutionally administer its tax system altogether without judicial intervention . . . the admitted absence of either civil or criminal jurisdiction would seem to dispose of the case."

This scolding was followed by repeating its earlier admonishment to Arizona in the *Williams v. Lee* case when it reiterated "This Court has therefore held that "the question has always been whether the state action infringed on the right of *reservation Indians* to make their own laws and be ruled by them"—In this case, appellant's rights as a reservation Indian were violated when the state collected a tax from her which it had no jurisdiction to impose."

The aforementioned cases deal with limitations on the states' authority to exercise jurisdiction on the reservations. The next section addresses the tribe's right to exercise civil jurisdiction in tribal courts. Prior to 1993, the Oglala Sioux Tribe exercised its civil jurisdiction under a tribal law that was an obstacle to tribal members with civil complaints against non-tribal members. The Law and Order Code, Chapter 2, Section 20 provided in part as follows:

"The Oglala Sioux tribal Court shall have jurisdiction of all suits wherein the defendant is a member of the tribe or tribes within their jurisdiction, and of all other suits between members and non-members which are brought by stipulation of both parties."

This ordinance had been adopted by the tribal council in the past and was very obstructive to tribal members, who had reason to file civil actions against non-members of the tribe. The law provided that non-members would have to "stipulate" to jurisdiction; whereas the tribal constitution was not so restrictive. The tribal Constitution, Article V. provided that the "judicial power shall extend to all cases involving only members of the Oglala Sioux Tribe, arising under the constitution and by-laws or ordinances of the Tribe, and to other cases in which all parties consent to jurisdiction."

The tribal code, which required non-tribal members to "stipulate" to jurisdiction prior to being sued, was far more restrictive than the tribal constitution, which required all parties to "consent" to jurisdiction.

In 1993, the tribal council addressed this problem, and decided that the constitutional provision requiring non-tribal members to consent to jurisdiction was far more beneficial to tribal members. The council decided to level the playing field for tribal members with civil complaints against nonmembers by defining "consent" to mean implied consent rather than by affirmative "stipulation".

Ordinance 93-12 now reads as follows:

NOW THEREFORE BE IT ORDAINED that paragraph 1, Chapter 2 Section 20 of the OST Law and Order Code is amended to read as follows:

Section 20. JURISDICITON

The Oglala Sioux Tribal Court shall have jurisdiction of all suits wherein the defendant is a member of the Oglala Sioux Tribe and of all other suits between members and non-members who consent to the jurisdiction of the tribe."

BE IT FURTHER ORDAINED that the Oglala Sioux Tribe does hereby adopt Section 20(a) and Section 20(b) of Chapter 2 as follows:

Section 20 (a) IMPLIED CONSENT TO TRIBAL JURISDICITON BY NON-MEMBERS OF THE OGLALA SIOUX TRIBE.

"Any person who is not a member of the Oglala Sioux Tribe shall be deemed as having consented to the jurisdiction of the Oglala Sioux Tribe by doing personally, through an employee, through an agent or through a subsidiary, any of the following acts within the exterior boundaries of the Pine Ridge Indian Reservation.

1. **The transaction of any business.**
2. **The commission or omission of any act which results in a tort action.**
3. **The ownership, use or possession of any property situated within the exterior boundaries of the Pine Ridge Indian Reservation.**
4. **Engaging in any employer-employee relationship.**
5. **Leasing or permitting of any land or property.**
6. **Residing on the Pine Ridge Indian Reservation.**
7. **Commission of any act giving rise to claims for spousal support, separate maintenance, child support child custody, divorce or modification of any decree of divorce or separate maintenance proceeding.**
8. **Any contractual agreement entered into within the exterior boundaries of the Pine Ridge Indian Reservation.**

This amended version of Section 20 allows tribal members to file lawsuits against non-members in tribal court without requiring non-members to expressly consent to jurisdiction. It is very puzzling why the original tribal ordinance was so restrictive, to the detriment of tribal members who had valid civil claims against non-members. The court contains no record of any non-member "stipulating" to jurisdiction, and many non-members are presently summoned into tribal court to face civil actions because they implicitly consent to jurisdiction.

Public Law 280.

Public Law 280, also known as the "Termination Law" was enacted on August 15, 1953. (Statutes at Large, LXVII, pp. 580-90)

The law conferred civil and criminal jurisdiction on five states, and allowed other states to assume jurisdiction over offenses committed by or against Indians on reservations within those states. The states were allowed to assume jurisdiction by amending their constitutions to extend state civil and criminal jurisdiction over Indian reservations.

Public Las 280 provides as follows:

"To Confer Jurisdiction on the Sates of California, Minnesota, Nebraska, Oregon, and Wisconsin with Respect to Criminal Offenses and Civil Causes of Action Committed or Arising on Indian Reservations within such States and for Other Purposes."

Sec. 1102. State jurisdiction over offenses committed by or against Indians in the Indian county.

"(a) Each of the States listed in the following table shall have jurisdiction over offenses committed by or against Indians in the areas of Indian country listed opposite the name of the State to the same extent that such State has jurisdiction over offenses committed elsewhere within the State, and the criminal laws of such State shall have the same force and effect within such Indian country as they have elsewhere within the State:

State of	Indian country affected
California	All Indian country within the State
Minnesota	All Indian country within the State, except the Red Lake Reservation.
Nebraska	All Indian country within the State
Oregon	All Indian country within the State, except the Warm Springs Reservation
Wisconsin	All Indian country within the State, except the Menominee Reservation.

"(b) Nothing in this section shall authorize the alienation, encumbrance, or taxation of any real or personal property, including water rights, belonging to any Indian or any Indian tribe, band, or community that is held in trust by the United States or shall authorize regulation of the use of such property in a manner inconsistent with any Federal treaty, agreement, or statute or within any regulation made pursuant thereto; or shall deprive any Indian or any Indian tribe, band or community of any right, privilege, or immunity afforded under Federal treaty, agreement, or statute with respect to hunting, trapping, or fishing or the control, licensing, or regulation thereof . . .

The provisions of sections 1152 and 1153 of this chapter shall not be applicable within the areas of Indian country listed in subsection (a) of this section."

A subsequent section allowed states not named in P.L. 280 to assume jurisdiction over Indian country by taking affirmative legislative action. The states were allowed to amend, **"where necessary their State constitution or existing statutes, as the case may be, to remove any legal impediment to the assumption of civil and criminal jurisdiction in accordance with the provisions of this Act;** *Provided,* **That the provisions of this Act shall not become effective with respect to such assumption of jurisdiction by any such state until the people thereof have appropriately amended their State constitution or statutes as the case may be."**

Section VII of the Act provided that:

"The consent of the United States is hereby given to any other State not having jurisdiction with respect to criminal offenses or civil causes of action, or with respect to both, as provided for in this Act, to assume jurisdiction at such time and in such manner as the people of the State shall, by affirmative legislative action, obligate and bind the State to assumption thereof."

Fifteen years later, in 1968, Congress passed the Indian Civil Rights Act, which amended PL. 280 to require the consent of the Tribe before any state could assume civil or criminal jurisdiction over Indian reservations. The landmark case interpreting P. L. 280 is *Kennerly v. District Court of Montana.*

KENNERLY v. DISTRICT COURT OF MONTANA, Supreme Court of the United States, 1973, 400 U.S. 423, 91 S. Ct. 480.

In 1967, the Blackfeet Tribe of Browning, Montana, enacted a tribal resolution stating that the "Tribal court and the State shall have concurrent and not exclusive jurisdiction of all suits wherein the defendant is a member of the Tribe."

Kennerly, who was a member of the Blackfeet Tribe, was sued in State court over debts for food bought on credit from a grocery store on the reservation. He challenged the jurisdiction of the state court. The Montana Supreme Court found that the actions of the Montana Supreme Court were consistent with the tribal resolution, and therefore did not interfere with the right of Indians to make their own laws and be governed by them. The United States Supreme Court reversed the Montana Supreme Court on grounds that Montana had not amended its constitution to legally assume jurisdiction over the reservation as required by P. L. 280. The federal law required "affirmative" state action, that is, state law would have to be enacted to assume jurisdiction and the state may not rely on a tribal resolution for authority to acquire jurisdiction over Indian country.

Kennerly stands for the rule of law that a tribal council may not grant the state jurisdiction by political action. The decision to allow a state to assume jurisdiction on the reservation is in the hands of the people. The tribal members, for example, must vote in a Secretarial election to transfer jurisdiction to the state. The election must address the single question of state jurisdiction in a public referendum election called by the Secretary of the Interior. At this point, it would be virtually impossible for a state to assume jurisdiction over Indian reservations given the current policy of Indian Self Determination, which grants the final choice to tribal members.

CHAPTER TEN

Treaty Interpretations

Treaty rights of tribal members sometimes conflict with state interests. When a tribal member exercising treaty rights encounters a state official that obstructs the tribal member, the matter can end up in either state or federal court. The following cases are some examples.

STATE v TINNO, Supreme Court of Idaho, 1972. 94 Idaho 759.

Gerald Cleo Tinno was a member of the Shoshone-Bannock Tribes, who resided on the Fort Hall Indian Reservation near Pocatello, Idaho. He was charged with taking a Chinook salmon with a spear from the Yankee Fork of the Salmon River on July 16, 1968. Spear fishing and taking salmon at that time and location were violations of state fishing regulations.

At trial, Tinno argued his right to fish was reserved in the Fort Bridger Treaty, which was made between the Shoshone-Bannock Tribes and the United States. The lower state court agreed with Tinno and the State of Idaho appealed to the Supreme Court of Idaho.

On appeal, the high court reviewed Article 4 of the treaty which reads: "The Indians herein named agree, when the agency house and other buildings shall be constructed on their reservations named, they will make said reservations their permanent home and they will make no permanent settlement elsewhere; but they shall have *the right to hunt on the unoccupied lands of the United States* so long as peace subsists among the whites and Indians on the borders of the *hunting districts.*"

The state argued that the treaty reserved the right to hunt, but not to fish. The court relied on the expert testimony of Dr. Sven S. Liljeblad, a professor of anthropology and linguistics at Idaho State University. According to Dr. Liljeblad, the term "to hunt" as used in the languages of the tribes was a verb that was not separated from hunting or fishing. The Shoshone verb and the Bannock verb both had the same meaning as to "obtain wild food". There was no distinction between hunting for food, or fishing for food, or other means of obtaining wild food. The court concluded, "As Dr. Liljeblad explained, the English terminology when translated to those Indian leaders at the treaty negotiations would have been understood to encompass both "fishing" and "hunting" for game." The Court endorsed the construction of the treaty, as did the district judge in his memorandum opinion:

> "There is no plausible reason why a traditional and basic means of subsistence of the Indian, the taking of fish, would not have been intended to be reserved by the Indian, or was intended to be extinguished by acquisition by the United States, while at the same time the Indians reserved the right to hunt all other foods. Since the treaty, the Indians have continued to take fish in the manner and the places taught and shown them by their forefathers. The history of the Indians, the tenor of the treaty, and the understanding of the treaty by the parties, dictate that the words 'to hunt' be not so delimited as to exclude the right 'to fish' . . ."

The Idaho State Supreme Court upheld the decision of the district court, which concluded that Tinno was exempt from all state regulation unless the state could show that such regulation was reasonably necessary to preserve the fish, which the state had failed to do.

WINTERS v. UNITED STATES, Supreme Court of the United States, 1908. 207 U.S. 564.

The Fort Belknap Reservation in Montana was set apart by Congress in 1874 for the Gros Ventre, Piegan Blood, Blackfeet, and River Crow Indians. The reservation was diminished to the Fort Belknap Reservation in 1888, wherein the northern boundary of the reservation was described as the middle of the Milk River, which runs through the Fort Belknap reservation. In 1895, white farmers settled upstream of the river and began diverting water from the Milk River, thus depriving tribal members access to the Milk River for irrigation purposes. In this case, it was the United States who sued the farmers on behalf of the Blackfeet Tribal members who occupied the Fort Belknap Reservation.

The agreement did not specifically address water rights of the Indians, and the farmers argued that the Indians made no reservation of waters. The Supreme Court decided that the Government had reserved the waters for the Indians relative to the purpose of the reservations—to change the habits of the Indians from roaming and hunting to a pastoral and civilized life of agriculture. The court reasoned that it would make no sense for the Government to establish the reservation, require Indians to select land allotments for farming, and not reserve necessary water in a dry area of the country. Without a reservation of water, the land in that part of the country would be useless for agricultural purposes. The Court cited a general rule of treaty interpretation, which applied in this case. "By a rule of interpretation of agreements and treaties with the Indians, ambiguities occurring will be resolved from the standpoint of the Indians." The effect of this case means that Indian tribes have at least an "implied" reservation of water if the treaty is silent on the subject. The "Winters Doctrine" as it is called, exemplifies a rare case in which the Government sides with the Indians against non-Indian citizens who are coveting Indian property. This case also represents the unusual result wherein the Indians actually acquired a return of property as opposed to a monetary judgment. For example, the Black Hills case was decided in favor of the Lakota nations, but there was no return of the property that was unconstitutionally taken. The Court of Claims was authorized to award monetary damages only for the loss of Indian property, and the property itself could not be returned to the rightful owner because of the statutes that established the legal basis for the claim. While the Lakota nations have a legal, moral, and ethical claim to the Black Hills, the court was not authorized to order a return of the property, as in the Winters case. Water rights and fishing rights are forms of property, which the Indian tribes have been able to retain. When a case involves land, however, it is rare for an Indian tribe to recover property, because the government commonly opposes the tribes and, of course, federal courts exclusively manage Indian land cases.

SANTA CLARA PUEBLO v. MARTINEZ, 439 U. S. 49 (1978)

The Indian Civil Rights Act is modeled after the U.S. Bill of Rights. Most of the civil rights and liberties are included in the ICRA, except for those federal rights that are inconsistent with tribal cultural traditions. For example, the federal prohibition of recognizing an established religion does not apply to Indian tribes. It is permissible for an Indian tribe to recognize and acknowledge religious activities that are not allowed in jurisdictions off the reservation.

The Santa Clara Pueblo is located in northern New Mexico and is home to over 1200 members of the pueblo. The pueblo adopted an enrollment code that allowed children of male tribal members to be enrolled and the children of female tribal members were eligible for enrollment provided that the father of the children was enrolled in the pueblo. Mrs. Julia Martinez, a full-blooded member of the pueblo, was married to a Navajo Indian. Consequently, her children were not allowed to be enrolled in her pueblo despite the fact that the children were born on the pueblo, grew up in the pueblo, spoke the Tewa language, and culturally identified themselves as members of the pueblo. The Supreme Court, in reviewing her challenge to the Santa Clara Pueblo enrollment code, decided that the case could not be heard in federal court because the ICRA did not vest the federal courts with jurisdiction to determine the rights of tribal members. Ms. Martinez argued that the Pueblo discriminated against her on the bases of gender, and therefore denied her the equal protection of law that is provided for in Section 8 of the ICRA.

The Supreme Court dismissed her complaint by ruling that there was no federal jurisdiction to determine the civil rights of Indians under the ICRA. The Court reasoned that the ICRA was intended to serve as a guide to tribal courts, and that the only federal remedy provided in the law is Section 1303—habeas corpus. The decision stands for the rule of law that violations of the ICRA by tribal governments should be adjudicated in tribal court, and that the policy of strengthening tribal courts requires the federal courts to defer such cases to tribal court.

APPENDIX A

TRIBAL LAW AND ORDER CODE

The Tribal Council has been passing laws and adopting ordinances for more than seventy years. The Tribal Law and Order Code is continually being revised to keep up with changing times, changing environments and changing economic and social conditions of the Tribe.

Following is a partial list of tribal ordinances found in the Oglala Sioux Tribal Law and Order Code.

Composition of the Court
Rules of Civil Procedure
Foreclosure Procedures
Domestic Relations
Dependent, Neglected or Delinquent Children Code
Juvenile Code
Adoption Requirements
Child Abuse and Neglect
Elder Abuse Code
Heirship—Probate
Criminal Procedures
Penal Code
Removal of Non-Members
Extradition Law
Taxation Provisions
Rules of Court
Grand Jury Ordinance
Motor vehicle code
Enrollment Code
OST Personnel Policies and Procedures
Tribal Employment Rights Ordinance

Administrative Operating Procedures
Records Management
Freedom of Information
Parade Ordinance
Zoning Code
Historic Site Preservation Code
Nuisance Abatement code
Education Code
Election Ordinance
Food Services Code
Gaming Code
Animal Control Code
Livestock Code
Water Ordinance
Sewer and sewage Ordinance
Garbage and Refuse Disposal
Grazing Ordinance
Fish and Wildlife
Motor Vehicle licensing
Mining Code
Oil and Gas Regulations
Oil and Gas Tax Severance
Timber Cutting Permits
Coroner of the Oglala Sioux Tribe
Reservation-Wide School Board
Fee Schedule for OST Business Licenses
Oglala Sioux tribal Bar Association
Oglala Sioux Tribal Leasehold Mortgages
OST Employment Fee Code
OST Fireworks Code

APPENDIX B

FORT LARAMIE TREATY, 1868

ARTICLES OF A TREATY MADE AND CONCLUDED BY AND BETWEEN

Lieutenant General William T. Sherman, General William S. Harney, General Alfred H. Terry, General O. O. Augur, J. B. Henderson, Nathaniel G. Taylor, John G. Sanborn, and Samuel F. Tappan, duly appointed commissioners on the part of the United States, and the different bands of the Sioux Nation of Indians, by their chiefs and headmen, whose names are hereto subscribed, they being duly authorized to act in the premises.

ARTICLE I. From this day forward all war between the parties to this agreement shall for ever cease. The government of the United States desires peace, and its honor is hereby pledged to keep it. The Indians desire peace, and they now pledge their honor to maintain it.

If bad men among the whites, or among other people subject to the authority of the United States, shall commit any wrong upon the person or property of the Indians, the United States will, upon proof made to the agent, and forwarded to the Commissioner of Indian Affairs at Washington city, proceed at once to cause the offender to be arrested and punished according to the laws of the United States, and also reimburse the injured person for the loss sustained.

If bad men among the Indians shall commit a wrong or depredation upon the person or property of nay one, white, black, or Indian, subject to the authority of the United States, and at peace therewith, the Indians herein named solemnly agree that they will, upon proof made to their agent, and notice by him, deliver up the wrongdoer to the United States, to be tried and punished according to its laws, and, in case they willfully refuse so to do, the person injured shall be reimbursed for his loss from the annuities, or other moneys due or to become due to them under this or other treaties made with the United States; and the President, on advising with the Commissioner of Indian Affairs, shall prescribe such rules and regulations for ascertaining damages under the provisions of this article as in his judgment may be proper, but no one sustaining loss while violating the provisions of this treaty, or the laws of the United States, shall be reimbursed therefore.

ARTICLE II. The United States agrees that the following district of country, to wit, viz: commencing on the east bank of the Missouri river where the 46th parallel of north latitude crosses the same, thence along low-water mark down said east bank to a point opposite where the northern line of the State of Nebraska strikes the river, thence west across said river, and along the northern line of Nebraska to the 104th degree of longitude west from Greenwich, thence north on said meridian to a point where the 46th parallel of north latitude intercepts the same, thence due east along said parallel to the place of beginning; and in addition thereto, all existing reservations of the east back of said river, shall be and the same is, set apart for the absolute and undisturbed use and occupation of the Indians herein named, and for such other friendly tribes or individual Indians as from time to time they may be willing, with the consent of the United States, to admit amongst them; and the United States now solemnly agrees that no persons, except those herein designated and authorized so to do, and except such officers, agents, and employees of the government as may be authorized to enter upon Indian reservations in discharge of duties enjoined by law, shall ever be permitted to pass over, settle upon, or reside in the territory described in this article, or in such territory as may be added to this reservation for the use of said Indians, and henceforth they will and do hereby relinquish all claims or right in and to any portion of the United States or Territories, except such as is embraced within the limits aforesaid, and except as hereinafter provided.

ARTICLE III. If it should appear from actual survey or other satisfactory examination of said tract of land that it contains less than 160 acres of tillable land for each person who, at the time, may be authorized to reside on it under the provisions of this treaty, and a very considerable number of such persons shall be disposed to commence cultivating the soil as farmers, the United States agrees to set apart, for the use of said Indians, as herein provided, such additional quantity of arable land, adjoining to said reservation, or as near to the same as it can be obtained, as may be required to provide the necessary amount.

ARTICLE IV. The United States agrees, at its own proper expense, to construct, at some place on the Missouri river, near the centre of said reservation where timber and water may be convenient, the following buildings, to wit, a warehouse, a store-room for the use of the agent in storing goods belonging to the Indians, to cost not less than $2,500; an agency building, for the residence of the agent, to cost not exceeding $3,000; a residence for the physician, to cost not more than $3,000; and five other buildings, for a carpenter, farmer, blacksmith, miller, and engineer-each to cost not exceeding $2,000;

also, a school-house, or mission building, so soon as a sufficient number of children can be induced by the agent to attend school, which shall not cost exceeding $5,000.

The United States agrees further to cause to be erected on said reservation, near the other buildings herein authorized, a good steam circular saw-mill, with a grist-mill and shingle machine attached to the same, to cost not exceeding $8,000.

ARTICLE V. The United States agrees that the agent for said Indians shall in the future make his home at the agency building; that he shall reside among them, and keep an office open at all times for the purpose of prompt and diligent inquiry into such matters of complaint by and against the Indians as may be presented for investigation under the provisions of their treaty stipulations, as also for the faithful discharge of other duties enjoined on him by law. In all cases of depredation on person or property he shall cause the evidence to be taken in writing and forwarded, together with his findings, to the Commissioner of Indian Affairs, whose decision, subject to the revision of the Secretary of the Interior, shall be binding on the parties to this treaty.

ARTICLE VI. If any individual belonging to said tribes of Indians, or legally incorporated with them, being the head of a family, shall desire to commence farming, he shall have the privilege to select, in the presence and with the assistance of the agent then in charge, a tract of land within said reservation, not exceeding three hundred and twenty acres in extent, which tract, when so selected, certified, and recorded in the "Land Book" as herein directed, shall cease to be held in common, but the same may be occupied and held in the exclusive possession of the person selecting it, and of his family, so long as he or they may continue to cultivate it.

Any person over eighteen years of age, not being the head of a family, may in like manner select and cause to be certified to him or her, for purposes of cultivation, a quantity of land, not exceeding eighty acres in extent, and thereupon be entitled to the exclusive possession of the same as above directed.

For each tract of land so selected a certificate, containing a description thereof and the name of the person selecting it, with a certificate endorsed thereon that the same has been recorded, shall be delivered to the party entitled to it, by the agent, after the same shall have been recorded by him in a book to be kept in his office, subject to inspection, which said book shall be known as the "Sioux Land Book."

The President may, at any time, order a survey of the reservation, and, when so surveyed, Congress shall provide for protecting the rights of said settlers in their improvements, and may fix the character of the title held by each. The United States may pass such laws on the subject of alienation and descent of property between the Indians and their descendants as may be thought proper. And it is further stipulated that any male Indians over eighteen years of age, of any band or tribe that is or shall hereafter become a party to this treaty, who now is or who shall hereafter become a resident or occupant of any reservation or territory not included in the tract of country designated and described in this treaty for the permanent home of the Indians, which is not mineral land, nor reserved by the United States for special purposes other than Indian occupation, and who shall have made improvements thereon of the value of two hundred dollars or more, and continuously occupied the same as a homestead for the term of three years, shall be entitled to receive from the United States a patent for one hundred and sixty acres of land including his said improvements, the same to be in the form of the legal subdivisions of the surveys of the public lands. Upon application in writing, sustained by the proof of two disinterested witnesses, made to the register of the local land office when the land sought to be entered is within a land district, and when the tract sought to be entered is not in any land district, then upon said application and proof being made to the Commissioner of the General Land Office, and the right of such Indian or Indians to enter such tract or tracts of land shall accrue and be perfect from the date of his first improvements thereon, and shall continue as long as he continues his residence and improvements and no longer. And any Indian or Indians receiving a patent for land under the foregoing provisions shall thereby and from thenceforth become and be a citizen of the United States and be entitled to all the privileges and immunities of such citizens, and shall, at the same time, retain all his rights to benefits accruing to Indians under this treaty.

ARTICLE VII. In order to insure the civilization of the Indians entering into this treaty, the necessity of education is admitted, especially of such of them as are or may be settled on said agricultural reservations, and they, therefore, pledge themselves to compel their children, male and female, between the ages of six and sixteen years, to attend school, and it is hereby made the duty of the agent for said Indians to see that this stipulation is strictly complied with; and the United States agrees that for every thirty children between said ages, who can be induced or compelled to attend school, a house shall be provided, and a teacher competent to teach the elementary branches of an English education shall be furnished, who will reside among said Indians and faithfully discharge his or her duties as a teacher. The provisions of this article to continue for not less than twenty years.

ARTICLE VIII. When the head of a family or lodge shall have selected lands and received his certificate as above directed, and the agent shall be satisfied that he intends in good faith to commence cultivating the soil for a living, he shall be entitled to receive seeds and agricultural implements for the first year, not exceeding in value one hundred dollars, and for each succeeding year he shall continue to farm, for a period of three years more, he shall be entitled to receive seeds and implements as aforesaid, not exceeding in value twenty-five dollars. And it is further stipulated that such persons as commence farming shall receive instruction from the farmer herein provided for, and whenever more than one hundred persons shall enter upon the cultivation of the soil, a second blacksmith shall be provided, with such iron, steel, and other material as may be needed.

ARTICLE IX. At any time after ten years from the making of this treaty, the United States shall have the privilege of withdrawing the physician, farmer, blacksmith, carpenter, engineer, and miller herein provided for, but in case of such withdrawal, an additional sum thereafter of ten thousand dollars per annum shall be devoted to the education of said Indians, and the Commissioner of Indian Affairs shall, upon careful inquiry into their condition, make such rules and regulations for the expenditure of said sums as will best promote the education and moral improvement of said tribes.

ARTICLE X. In lieu of all sums of money or other annuities provided to be paid to the Indians herein named under any treaty or treaties heretofore made, the United States agrees to deliver at the agency house on the reservation herein named, on or before the first day of August of each year, for thirty years, the following articles, to wit:

For each male person over 14 years of age, a suit of good substantial woolen clothing, consisting of coat, pantaloons, flannel shirt, hat, and a pair of home-made socks.

For each female over 12 years of age, a flannel shirt, or the goods necessary to make it, a pair of woolen hose, 12 yards of calico, and 12 yards of cotton domestics.

For the boys and girls under the ages named, such flannel and cotton goods as may be needed to make each a suit as aforesaid, together with a pair of woolen hose for each.

And in order that the Commissioner of Indian Affairs may be able to estimate properly for the articles herein named, it shall be the duty of the agent each year to forward to him a full and exact census of the Indians, on which the estimate from year to year can be based.

And in addition to the clothing herein named, the sum of $10 for each person entitled to the beneficial effects of this treaty shall be annually appropriated for a period of 30 years, while such persons roam and hunt, and $20 for each person who engages in farming, to be used by the Secretary of the Interior in the purchase of such articles as from time to time the condition and necessities of the Indians may indicate to be proper. And if within the 30 years, at any time, it shall appear that the amount of money needed for clothing, under this article, can be appropriated to better uses for the Indians named herein, Congress may, by law, change the appropriation to other purposes, but in no event shall the amount of the appropriation be withdrawn or discontinued for the period named. And the President shall annually detail an officer of the army to be present and attest the delivery of all the goods herein named, to the Indians, and he shall inspect and report on the quantity and quality of the goods and the manner of their delivery. And it is hereby expressly stipulated that each Indian over the age of four years, who shall have removed to and settled permanently upon said reservation, one pound of meat and one pound of flour per day, provided the Indians cannot furnish their own subsistence at an earlier date. And it is further stipulated that the United States will furnish and deliver to each lodge of Indians or family of persons legally incorporated with the, who shall remove to the reservation herein described and commence farming, one good American cow, and one good well-broken pair of American oxen within 60 days after such lodge or family shall have so settled upon said reservation.

ARTICLE XI. In consideration of the advantages and benefits conferred by this treaty and the many pledges of friendship by the United States, the tribes who are parties to this agreement hereby stipulate that they will relinquish all right to occupy permanently the territory outside their reservations as herein defined, but yet reserve the right to hunt on any lands north of North Platte, and on the Republican Fork of the Smoky Hill river, so long as the buffalo may range thereon in such numbers as to justify the chase. And they, the said Indians, further expressly agree:

1st. That they will withdraw all opposition to the construction of the railroads now being built on the plains.

2d. That they will permit the peaceful construction of any railroad not passing over their reservation as herein defined.

3d. That they will not attack any persons at home, or travelling, nor molest or disturb any wagon trains, coaches, mules, or cattle belonging to the people of the United States, or to persons friendly therewith.

4th. They will never capture, or carry off from the settlements, white women or children.

5th. They will never kill or scalp white men, nor attempt to do them harm.

6th. They withdraw all pretence of opposition to the construction of the railroad now being built along the Platte river and westward to the Pacific ocean, and they will not in future object to the construction of railroads, wagon roads, mail stations, or other works of utility or necessity, which may be ordered or permitted by the laws of the United States. But should such roads or other works be constructed on the lands of their reservation, the government will pay the tribe whatever amount of damage may be assessed by three disinterested commissioners to be appointed by the President for that purpose, one of the said commissioners to be a chief or headman of the tribe.

7th. They agree to withdraw all opposition to the military posts or roads now established south of the North Platte river, or that may be established, not in violation of treaties heretofore made or hereafter to be made with any of the Indian tribes.

ARTICLE XII. No treaty for the cession of any portion or part of the reservation herein described which may be held in common, shall be of any validity or force as against the said Indians unless executed and signed by at least three-fourths of all the adult male Indians occupying or interested in the same, and no cession by the tribe shall be understood or construed in such manner as to deprive, without his consent, any individual member of the tribe of his rights to any tract of land selected by him as provided in Article VI of this treaty.

ARTICLE XIII. The United States hereby agrees to furnish annually to the Indians the physician, teachers, carpenter, miller, engineer, farmer, and blacksmiths, as herein contemplated, and that such appropriations shall be made from time to time, on the estimate of the Secretary of the Interior, as will be sufficient to employ such persons.

ARTICLE XIV. It is agreed that the sum of five hundred dollars annually for three years from date shall be expended in presents to the ten persons of said tribe who in the judgment of the agent may grow the most valuable crops for the respective year.

ARTICLE XV. The Indians herein named agree that when the agency house and other buildings shall be constructed on the reservation named, they will regard said reservation their permanent home, and they will make no permanent settlement elsewhere; but they shall have the right, subject to the conditions and modifications of this treaty, to hunt, as stipulated in Article XI hereof.

ARTICLE XVI. The United States hereby agrees and stipulates that the country north of the North Platte river and east of the summits of the Big Horn mountains shall be held and considered to be unceded. Indian territory, and also stipulates and agrees that no white person or persons shall be permitted to settle upon or occupy any portion of the same; or without the consent of the Indians, first had and obtained, to pass through the same; and it is further agreed by the United States, that within ninety days after the conclusion of peace with all the bands of the Sioux nation, the military posts now established in the territory in this article named shall be abandoned, and that the road leading to them and by them to the settlements in the Territory of Montana shall be closed.

ARTICLE XVII. It is hereby expressly understood and agreed by and between the respective parties to this treaty that the execution of this treaty and its ratification by the United States Senate shall have the effect, and shall be construed as abrogating and annulling all treaties and agreements heretofore entered into between the respective parties hereto, so far as such treaties and agreements obligate the United States to furnish and provide money, clothing, or other articles of property to such Indians and bands of Indians as become parties to this treaty, but no further.

In testimony of all which, we, the said commissioners, and we, the chiefs and headmen of the Brule band of the Sioux nation, have hereunto set our hands and seals at Fort Laramie, Dakota Territory, this twenty-ninth day of April, in the year one thousand eight hundred and sixty-eight.

N. G. TAYLOR,

W. T. SHERMAN, Lieutenant General

WM. S. HARNEY, Brevet Major General U.S.A.

JOHN B. SANBORN,

S. F. TAPPAN,

C. C. AUGUR, Brevet Major General

ALFRED H. TERRY, Brevet Major General U.S.A.

Attest:

A. S. H. WHITE, Secretary.

Executed on the part of the Brule band of Sioux by the chiefs and headman whose names are hereto annexed, they being thereunto duly authorized, at Fort Laramie, D. T., the twenty-ninth day of April, in the year A. D. 1868.

MA-ZA-PON-KASKA, his X mark, Iron Shell.

WAH-PAT-SHAH, his X mark, Red Leaf.

HAH-SAH-PAH, his X mark, Black Horn.

ZIN-TAH-GAH-LAT-WAH, his X mark, Spotted Tail.

ZIN-TAH-GKAH, his X mark, White Tail.

ME-WAH-TAH-NE-HO-SKAH, his X mark, Tall Man.

SHE-CHA-CHAT-KAH, his X mark, Bad Left Hand.

NO-MAH-NO-PAH, his X mark, Two and Two.

TAH-TONKA-SKAH, his X mark, White Bull.

CON-RA-WASHTA, his X mark, Pretty Coon.

HA-CAH-CAH-SHE-CHAH, his X mark, Bad Elk.

WA-HA-KA-ZAH-ISH-TAH, his X mark, Eye Lance.

MA-TO-HA-KE-TAH, his X mark, Bear that looks behind.

BELLA-TONKA-TONKA, his X mark, Big Partisan.

MAH-TO-HO-HONKA, his X mark, Swift Bear.

TO-WIS-NE, his X mark, Cold Place.

ISH-TAH-SKAH, his X mark, White Eye.

MA-TA-LOO-ZAH, his X mark, Fast Bear.

AS-HAH-HAH-NAH-SHE, his X mark, Standing Elk.

CAN-TE-TE-KI-YA, his X mark, The Brave Heart.

SHUNKA-SHATON, his X mark, Day Hawk.

TATANKA-WAKON, his X mark, Sacred Bull.

MAPIA SHATON, his X mark, Hawk Cloud.

MA-SHA-A-OW, his X mark, Stands and Comes.

SHON-KA-TON-KA, his X mark, Big Dog.

Attest:

ASHTON S. H. WHITE, Secretary of Commission.

GEORGE B. WITHS, Phonographer to Commission.

GEO. H. HOLTZMAN.

JOHN D. HOWLAND.

JAMES C. O'CONNOR.

CHAR. E. GUERN, Interpreter.

LEON T. PALLARDY, Interpreter.

NICHOLAS JANIS, Interpreter.

Executed on the part of the Ogallalla band of Sioux by the chiefs and headmen whose names are hereto subscribed, they being thereunto duly authorized, at Fort Laramie, the 25th day of May, in the year A. D. 1868.

TAH-SHUN-KA-CO-QUI-PAH, his + mark,

Man-afraid-of-his-horses.

SHA-TON-SKAH, his + mark, White Hawk.

SHA-TON-SAPAH, his + mark, Black Hawk.

EGA-MON-TON-KA-SAPAH, his + mark, Black Tiger

OH-WAH-SHE-CHA, his + mark, Bad Wound.

PAH-GEE, his + mark, Grass.

WAH-NON SAH-CHE-GEH, his + mark, Ghost Heart.

COMECH, his + mark, Crow.

OH-HE-TE-KAH, his + mark, The Brave.

TAH-TON-KAH-HE-YO-TA-KAH, his + mark, Sitting Bull.

SHON-KA-OH-WAH-MEN-YE, his + mark, Whirlwind Dog.

HA-KAH-KAH-TAH-MIECH, his + mark, Poor Elk.

WAM-BU-LEE-WAH-KON, his + mark, Medicine Eagle.

CHON-GAH-MA-HE-TO-HANS-KA, his + mark, High Wolf.

WAH-SECHUN-TA-SHUN-KAH, his + mark, American Horse.

MAH-KAH-MAH-HA-MAK-NEAR, his + mark,

Man that walks under the ground.

MAH-TO-TOW-PAH, his + mark, Four Bears.

MA-TO-WEE-SHA-KTA, his + mark,

One that kills the bear.

OH-TAH-KEE-TOKA-WEE-CHAKTA, his + mark,

One that kills in a hard place.

TAH-TON-KAH-TA-MIECH, his + mark, The Poor Bull.

OH-HUNS-EE-GA-NON-SKEN, his + mark, Mad Shade.

SHAH-TON-OH-NAH-OM-MINNE-NE-OH-MINNE, his + mark, Whirling hawk.

MAH-TO-CHUN-KA-OH, his + mark, Bear's Back.

CHE-TON-WEE-KOH, his + mark, Fool Hawk.

WAH-HOH-KE-ZA-AH-HAH, his + mark,

EH-TON-KAH, his + mark, Big Mouth.

MA-PAH-CHE-TAH, his + mark, Bad Hand.

WAH-KE-YUN-SHAH, his + mark, Red Thunder.

WAK-SAH, his + mark, One that Cuts Off.

CHAH-NOM-QUI-YAH, his + mark,

One that Presents the Pipe.

WAH-KE-KE-YAN-PUH-TAH, his + mark, Fire Thunder.

MAH-TO-NONK-PAH-ZE, his + mark,

Bear with Yellow Ears.

CON-REE-TEH-KA, his + mark, The Little Crow.

HE-HUP-PAH-TOH, his + mark, The Blue War Club.

SHON-KEE-TOH, his + mark, The Blue Horse.

WAM-BALLA-OH-CONQUO, his + mark, Quick Eagle.

TA-TONKA-SUPPA, his + mark, Black Bull.

MOH-TOH-HA-SHE-NA, his + mark, The Bear Hide.

Attest:

S. E. WARD.

JAS. C. O'CONNOR.

J. M. SHERWOOD.

W. C. SLICER.

SAM DEON.

H. M. MATHEWS.

JOSEPH BISS

NICHOLAS JANIS, Interpreter.

LEFROY JOTT, Interpreter.

ANTOINE JANIS, Interpreter.

Executed on the part of the Minneconjou band of Sioux by the chiefs and headmen whose names are hereunto subscribed, they being thereunto duly authorized.

HEH-WON-GE-CHAT, his + mark, One Horn.

OH-PON-AH-TAH-E-MANNE, his + mark,

The Elk that Bellows Walking.

HEH-HO-LAH-ZEH-CHA-SKAH, his + mark,

Young White Bull.

WAH-CHAH-CHUM-KAH-COH-KEEPAH, his + mark,

One that is Afraid of Shield.

HE-HON-NE-SHAKTA, his + mark, The Old Owl.

MOC-PE-A-TOH, his + mark, Blue Cloud.

OH-PONG-GE-LE-SKAH, his + mark, Spotted Elk.

TAH-TONK-KA-HON-KE-SCHUE, his + mark, Slow Bull.

SHONK-A-NEE-SHAH-SHAH-ATAH-PE, his + mark,

The Dog Chief.

MA-TO-TAH-TA-TONK-KA, his + mark, Bull Bear.

WOM-BEH-LE-TON-KAH, his + mark, The Big Eagle.

MATOH, EH-SCHNE-LAH, his + mark, The Lone Bear.

MA-TOH-OH-HE-TO-KEH, his + mark, The Brave Bear.

EH-CHE-MA-KEH, his + mark, The Runner.

TI-KI-YA, his + mark, The Hard.

HE-MA-ZA, his + mark, Iron Horn.

Attest:

JAS. C O'CONNOR,

WM. D. BROWN,

NICHOLAS JANIS,

ANTOINE JANIS,

Interpreters.

Executed on the part of the Yanctonais band of Sioux by the chiefs and headmen whose names are hereto subscribed, they being thereunto duly authorized:

MAH-TO-NON-PAH, his + mark, Two Bears.

MA-TO-HNA-SKIN-YA, his + mark, Mad Bear.

HE-O-PU-ZA, his + mark, Louzy.

AH-KE-CHE-TAH-CHE-KA-DAN, his + mark, Little Soldier.

MAH-TO-E-TAN-CHAN, his + mark, Chief Bear.

CU-WI-TO-WIA, his + mark, Rotten Stomach.

SKUN-KA-WE-TKO, his + mark, Fool Dog.

ISH-TA-SAP-PAH, his + mark, Black Eye.

IH-TAN-CHAN, his + mark, The Chief.

I-A-WI-CA-KA, his + mark, The One who Tells the Truth.

AH-KE-CHE-TAH, his + mark, The Soldier.

TA-SHI-NA-GI, his + mark, Yellow Robe.

NAH-PE-TON-KA, his + mark, Big Hand.

CHAN-TEE-WE-KTO, his + mark, Fool Heart.

HOH-GAN-SAH-PA, his + mark, Black Catfish.

MAH-TO-WAH-KAN, his + mark, Medicine Bear.

SHUN-KA-KAN-SHA, his + mark, Red Horse.

WAN-RODE, his + mark, The Eagle.

CAN-HPI-SA-PA, his + mark, Black Tomahawk.

WAR-HE-LE-RE, his + mark, Yellow Eagle.

CHA-TON-CHE-CA, his + mark, Small Hawk, or Long Fare.

SHU-GER-MON-E-TOO-HA-SKA, his + mark, Fall Wolf.

MA-TO-U-TAH-KAH, his + mark, Sitting Bear.

HI-HA-CAH-GE-NA-SKENE, his + mark, Mad Elk.

Arapahoes.

LITTLE CHIEF, his + mark.

TALL BEAR, his + mark.

TOP MAN, his + mark.

NEVA, his + mark.

THE WOUNDED BEAR, his + mark.

WHIRLWIND, his + mark.

THE FOX, his + mark.

THE DOG BIG MOUTH, his + mark.

SPOTTED WOLF, his + mark.

SORREL HORSE, his + mark.

BLACK COAL, his + mark.

BIG WOLF, his + mark.

KNOCK-KNEE, his + mark.

BLACK CROW, his + mark.

THE LONE OLD MAN, his + mark.

PAUL, his + mark.

BLACK BULL, his + mark.

BIG TRACK, his + mark.

THE FOOT, his + mark.

BLACK WHITE, his + mark.

YELLOW HAIR, his + mark.

LITTLE SHIELD, his + mark.

BLACK BEAR, his + mark.

WOLF MOCASSIN, his + mark.

BIG ROBE, his + mark.

WOLF CHIEF, his + mark.

Witnesses:

ROBERT P. MCKIBBIN, Captain 4th Infantry, and Bvt. Lieut. Col. U. S. A., Commanding Fort Laramie.

WM. H. POWELL, Brevet Major, Captain 4th Infantry.

HENRY W. PATTERSON, Captain 4th Infantry.

THEO E. TRUE, Second Lieutenant 4th Infantry.

W. G. BULLOCK.

FORT LARAMIE, WYOMING TERRITORY November 6, 1868.

MAH-PI-AH-LU-TAH, his + mark, Red Cloud.

WA-KI-AH-WE-CHA-SHAH, his + mark, Thunder Man.

MA-ZAH-ZAH-GEH, his + mark, Iron Cane.

WA-UMBLE-WHY-WA-KA-TUYAH, his + mark, High Eagle.

KO-KE-PAH, his + mark, Man Afraid.

WA-KI-AH-WA-KOU-AH, his + mark, Thunder Flying Running.

Witnesses:

W. MCE. DYE, Brevet Colonel U. S. Army, Commanding.

A. B. CAIN, Captain 4th Infantry, Brevet Major U. S. Army.

ROBT. P. MCKIBBIN, Captain 4th Infantry, Bvt. Lieut. Col. U. S. Army.

JNO. MILLER, Captain 4th Infantry.

G. L. LUHN, First Lieutenant 4th Infantry, Bvt. Capt. U. S. Army.

H. C. SLOAN, Second Lieutenant 4th Infantry.

THE INDIAN CIVIL RIGHTS ACT OF 1968

THE INDIAN CIVIL RIGHTS ACT OF 1968 (ICRA) Federal Law 25 U.S.C. 1301-1303 provides as follows:

Sec. 1301. Definitions: For purposes of this subchapter, the term

1. "Indian tribe" means any tribe, band, or other group of Indians subject to the jurisdiction of the United States and recognized as possessing powers of self-government.
2. "powers of self-government" means and includes all governmental powers possessed by an Indian tribe, executive, legislative, and judicial, and all offices, bodies, and tribunals by and through which they are executed, including courts of Indian offenses; and means the inherent power of Indian tribes, hereby recognized and affirmed, to exercise criminal jurisdiction over all Indians;
3. "Indian court" means any Indian tribal court or court of Indian offenses, and,
4. "Indian" means any person who would be subject to the jurisdiction of the United States as an Indian under section 1153, title 19, United States Code, if that person were to commit an offense listed in that section in Indian country to which that section applies.

Sec. 1302. Constitutional Rights: **No Indian tribe** in exercising powers of self-government shall:

1. make or enforce any law prohibiting the free exercise of religion, or abridging the freedom of speech, or of the press, or the right of the people peaceably to assemble and to petition for a redress of grievances;
2. violate the right of the people to be secure in their persons, houses, papers, and effects against unreasonable search and seizures, nor issue warrants, but upon probable cause, supported by oath or affirmation, and particularly describing the place to be searched and the person or thing to be seized.

3. subject any person for the same offense to be twice put in jeopardy;

4. compel any person in any criminal case to be a witness against himself;

5. take any property for a public use without just compensation;

6. deny to any person in a criminal proceeding the right to a speedy and public trial, to be informed of the nature and cause of the accusation, to be confronted with the witnesses against him, to have compulsory process for obtaining witnesses in his favor, and at his own expense to have the assistance of counsel for his defense;

7. require excessive bail, impose excessive fines, inflict cruel and unusual punishments, and in no event impose for conviction of any one offense any penalty or punishment greater than imprisonment for a term of one year or a fine of $5,000 or both;

8. deny to any person within its jurisdiction the equal protection of its laws or deprive any person of liberty or property without due process of laws;

9. pass any bill of attainder or ex post facto law; or

10. deny to any person accused of an offense punishable by imprisonment the right, upon request, to a trial by jury of not less than six persons.

Section 1303—Habeas Corpus

The privilege of the writ of habeas corpus shall be available to any person, in a court of the United States, to test the legality of his detention by order of an Indian tribe.

GREAT SIOUX RESERVATION BOUNDARIES

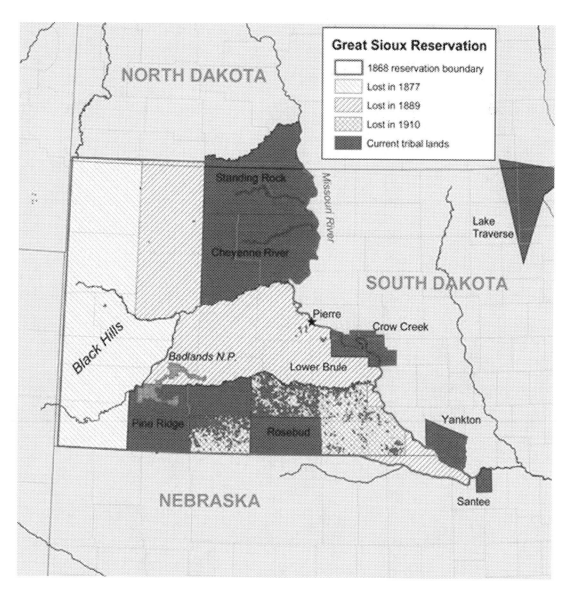

BIBLIOGAPHY

American Indian Treaty Making, Motives and Meanings
Raymond DeMallie, Institute for the Development of Indian Law,
Lawton, Oklahoma

Dakota Indian Treaties, From Nomad to Reservation
Don C. Clowser—Deadwood, SD

Come Black robe
John J. Killoren, S. J.

Black Hills, White Justice
Edward Lazarus

South Dakota
T. D. Griffith—Compass American Guides

Jake Herman Family Members

110 Cong. Record 12723 (1964)